Quilt a Gift
for Little Ones

Quilt a Gift
for Little Ones

22 heart-felt projects

Barri Sue Gaudet

D&C
David and Charles

www.rucraft.co.uk

A DAVID & CHARLES BOOK
© F&W Media International, LTD 2011

David & Charles is an imprint of F&W Media International, LTD
Brunel House, Forde Close, Newton Abbot, TQ12 4PU, UK

F&W Media International, LTD is a subsidiary of F+W Media, Inc.
4700 East Galbraith Road, Cincinnati, OH 45236

First published in the UK and USA in 2011

Text and designs © Barri Sue Gaudet 2011
Layout and photography © F&W Media International, LTD 2011

Barri Sue Gaudet has asserted her right to be identified as author
of this work in accordance with the Copyright, Designs and Patents
Act, 1988.

The author and publisher have made every effort to ensure that all
the instructions in the book are accurate and safe, and therefore
cannot accept liability for any resulting injury, damage or loss to
persons or property, however it may arise.

Names of manufacturers, fabric ranges and other products
are provided for the information of readers, with no intention
to infringe copyright or trademarks.

A catalogue record for this book is available from the
British Library.

ISBN-13: 978-0-7153-3866-7 paperback
ISBN-10: 0-7153-3866-8 paperback

Printed in China by RR Donnelley
for F&W Media International LTD,
Brunel House, Forde Close, Newton Abbot, TQ12 4PU, UK

10 9 8 7 6 5 4 3 2 1

Publisher Alison Myer
Senior Acquisitions Editor Cheryl Brown
Desk Editor Jeni Hennah
Project Editor Lin Clements
Senior Designer Jodie Lystor
Photographers Sian Irvine and Joe Giacomet
Senior Production Controller Kelly Smith

F+W Media Inc. publishes high quality books on a wide range
of subjects. For more great book ideas visit: **www.rucraft.co.uk**

Contents

Introduction

The anticipation of a new baby is the ideal
occasion for you to create a treasured first
gift. In this book you will find a collection of
items perfect for the baby's arrival. The projects
designed for the little one are suitable for a
variety of skill levels, from beginner through
to advanced. These special baby gifts include
techniques such as hand sewing, piecing by
machine, easy embroidery stitches or simple
appliqué. The gifts you create, whether it takes
an evening, a day or a week will be a delight
for the new family.

There are several gift-giving opportunities for all
stages of the pending arrival. A baby shower
is a fun time to surprise the new mum with
little necessities handmade by you to welcome
the little one. The baby will be precious
swaddled in a soft and pretty lined basket and
matching blanket. Mum is not forgotten with
a handy caddy to hold baby items. There are
projects for a brand new little boy or girl and
to get the nursery ready. These projects are
interchangeable and the motifs provided will fit
nicely into any decorating scheme.

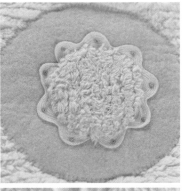

Many baby photographs are sure to be taken and there are gifts to hold keepsakes and snapshots in a lovely display. Grandmas are also included, with an overnight tote ready with necessities for the first visit to the new grandparents. Projects designed for learning and play include a soft throw, blocks and a book to touch and learn.

While this book is bundled for baby, you will also receive tips for embroidery stitches, techniques for fabric and wool felt appliqué and suggestions for using textured fabrics. There is plenty of help to assist your sewing and expand your capabilities while creating sweet treasured gifts for the little one.

There is nothing more exciting than the miracle of life and I hope these projects add to the joy of the event.

Welcome Baby

The projects in this chapter are perfect to celebrate the imminent arrival of a new baby into the family and you can make lovely gifts for mother and baby in no time at all. For a quick and easy present for a mum-to-be why not start with some wraps for a set of baby's bottles, perhaps filled with sweet treats for her? An adorable pair of little booties soft enough for a newborn baby is easy to create for a little girl or boy. A welcoming bunting hung with a pompom trim makes a lovely decoration for the nursery and can be made with stars and rocking horse appliqués for a baby boy or flowers and hearts for a baby girl.

The colour scheme in this chapter is a fresh, welcoming lemon, which mixes well with many other colours. Checks, spots and nursery-themed fabrics are combined with fusible web appliqué to create some lovely motifs from wool felt.

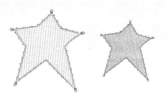

3 hour project

Bottle Wraps

These wraps are very easy to create and would make a wonderful gift to take to a baby shower. Two sizes are described here but you could easily change the sizes.

You will need...

- Yellow print fabric ¼yd (25cm)
- Fabric for appliqué (hearts or stars) 6in x 6in (15.2cm x 15.2cm)
- Wool felt for appliqué (pink or yellow) 5in x 5in (12.7cm x 12.7cm)
- Interfacing 4in x 9in (10.2cm x 23cm)
- Ric-rac for trim ⅝in x ¾yd (1.6cm x 75cm)
- Elastic ⅜in x 15in (1cm x 38.1cm)
- Embroidery stranded cotton (floss) to match appliqué fabrics or wool felts

For the large size:
- Fusible web and freezer paper

For the small size:
- DMC stranded cotton (floss) for flowers 152 pink, 470 green, 3821 yellow; for stars 813 blue, 3821 yellow, 3752 light blue and blanc (white)

Finished size:
Large: 4in x 7in (10.2cm x 17.8cm)

Small: 2¾in x 6½in (7cm x 16.5cm)

>> Directions

1 Cut the small wrap 4½in x 8in (11.4cm x 20.3cm). Cut the large wrap 7in x 8in (17.8cm x 20.3cm). For both sizes, turn under ¼in (6mm) along the long length for a hem. For the large wrap, turn under another 1⅝in (4.1cm) on both sides, so each piece is 3¼in x 8in (8.2cm x 20.3cm). For the small wrap, turn under another 1in (2.5cm) on both sides, so each piece is 2in x 8in (5cm x 20.3cm). Back both sizes with fusible interfacing, centring the interfacing in the middle and on the wrong side.

2 Using the relevant templates in the Templates section, add the appliqué on the large wraps by tracing the large stars or hearts on to fusible webbing. Press on to the back of the fabrics and cut out. Trace small stars or hearts on to freezer paper. Press on to wool felt and cut out. Fuse the motifs in place. Pin or glue wool felt stars or hearts in place. With one strand of matching stranded cotton, whipstitch the edges. On the stars work a French knot in blue cotton in the centre. Keep the linings open when sewing.

3 Work the embroidery on the small wraps as described in the panel, right.

4 To make up a wrap, mark the casing lines on the front, on both sizes, along the 8in (20.3cm) length, ⅝in (1.6cm) in from both edges. To sew together, open all folds. With right sides together, sew along the sides leaving gaps as shown in Fig 1. Press seams open.

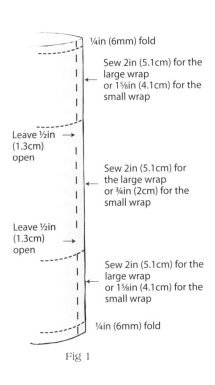

¼in (6mm) fold

Sew 2in (5.1cm) for the large wrap or 1⅝in (4.1cm) for the small wrap

Leave ½in (1.3cm) open →

Sew 2in (5.1cm) for the large wrap or ¾in (2cm) for the small wrap

Leave ½in (1.3cm) open →

Sew 2in (5.1cm) for the large wrap or 1⅝in (4.1cm) for the small wrap

¼in (6mm) fold

Fig 1

›› Embroidery

- Work the flower petals on the small wrap with two strands of pink cotton and lazy daisy stitch. Use green and lazy daisy stitch for the leaves. Add a French knot in yellow in the flower centres **(1)**.

- Backstitch the stars with two strands of blue and add a French knot in the centre. Add French knots for dots around the stars in yellow, blanc and light blue **(2)**.

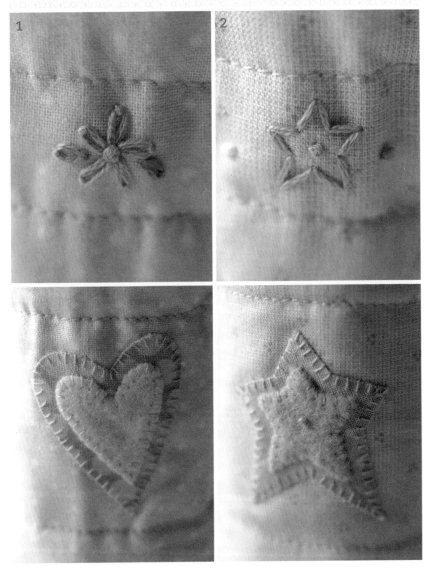

5 Turn all folds to the inside and whipstitch closed to cover the appliqué and embroidery stitches. Topstitch on the marked casing lines. Cut two lengths of ric-rac each 8in (20.3cm). Overlap the ends by ¼ in (6mm) and zigzag stitch to hold. Tack (baste) the ric-rac to the top and bottom and topstitch in place ¹⁄₁₆in (1.5mm) from the edge. Remove tacking (basting).

6 Cut elastic 6½in (16.5cm) long and work it through the opening in the seam, overlap the ends and whipstitch together. Work the elastic into the casing and whipstitch the opening. Remove marking lines to finish.

>> TIP

Put a safety pin on one end of the length of elastic to work it through the casing. When you are through to the other end, remove the pin.

 **2 day project**

Cutie Booties

These sweet little booties are so easy to create you'll want to make them for all the new babies you know! An ultra-soft lining makes them very comfortable to wear.

You will need...

- Yellow print fabric ⅛yd (12.5cm)
- Minkee or fleece for lining ⅛yd (12.5cm)
- Pink or blue fabric for appliqué (flowers or stars) 4in x 4in (10.2cm x 10.2cm)
- Yellow wool felt for appliqué 3in x 3in (7.6cm x 7.6cm)
- Fusible interfacing ½yd (50cm)
- Fusible web and freezer paper
- Ribbon ⅛in (3mm) x 12in (30.5cm)
- Embroidery cotton (floss) to match appliqué fabrics or wool felts

For girl booties:
- Green fabric for leaves appliqué 3in x 3in (7.6cm x 7.6cm)
- DMC embroidery cotton (floss) for flowers 152 pink, 470 green, 3821 light yellow and 3852 yellow

For boy booties:
- DMC embroidery cotton (floss) 813 blue, 3852 yellow and blanc (white)

Finished size:
Will fit newborn to one month old

 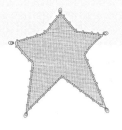

›› Directions

1 See the Template section at the back of the book for the relevant templates. Trace the sole, heel and toe templates on to the paper side of the freezer paper. The ¼in (6mm) seam allowance is included on the templates. Cut out the shapes.

2 Back the fleece with fusible interfacing to eliminate the stretch in the fabric. Back the fabric with interfacing for stability. Press the shiny side of the freezer paper templates on to the fabric and the fleece and trace the shapes. Cut out two soles, a right and a left. Cut out two toe and heel pieces. Trace the embroidery lines on to the fabric toe and heel pieces.

3 Work the appliqué on the toe pieces as follows. Trace the large stars or flowers on to fusible web. Press on the back of the fabrics and cut out. Trace the small stars or flowers on to freezer paper. Press on to yellow wool felt and cut out. Trace the leaves on to fusible web. Press on to the back of green fabrics and cut out six leaves. Fuse the flowers in place with three leaves tucked under. Fuse the stars in place. Pin or glue wool felt stars or flowers in place. Whipstitch in position with one strand of matching embroidery cotton.

4 Work the embroidery on the toe and heel pieces as described in the panel, right.

» Embroidery

- Work the embroidery on the toe piece using two strands of yellow embroidery cotton, with running stitch in a crescent shape. With pink cotton work a French knot in each flower centre. With blue cotton work a French knot in the centre of each star (1).
- Work most of the embroidery on the heel piece. For the girl booties use two strands of cotton and work pink lazy daisy petals and green leaves with a light yellow French knot in the middle of each flower. For the boy booties use two strands of cotton and work straight stitch in blue for stars (2).
- For both booties use three strands of white to work French knot dots between flowers or stars. Do not do the running stitch yet.

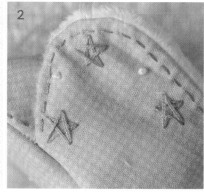

5 Pin or tack (baste) ribbon to the heel piece on the fabric where shown on the template. Let the ribbon extend ⅜in (1cm) to the inside for strength. With right sides together, sew the toe and heel pieces with one side fabric and one side fleece along the dotted sewing lines. Trim the seams but do not trim the ribbon. Clip to the seams at inside corners. Turn and press, making sure selvedge edges are even, trimming if necessary.

6 With a 1½in x 2in (3.8cm x 5.1cm) piece of fusible web, fuse the fabric sole to the fleece sole to hold together before sewing.

7 With right sides together (fabric to fabric) and starting with the heel, match heel ends to the lines indicated on each side of sole piece. Pin at the ends and at the centre of the heel. Starting at heel ends, sew a ¼in (6mm) seam from end to end around the heel side of the sole (see Fig 1). These are tiny, so push tucks away as you get to them. Do not turn.

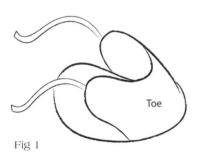

Fig 1

8 With right sides together, slightly overlap the toe piece over the heel piece just sewn. Pin at the ends and centre. Sew a ¼in (6mm) seam, keeping the ribbon ties out of the seam (Fig 2). Trim all around and turn right side out. Push out the sole piece and press seams.

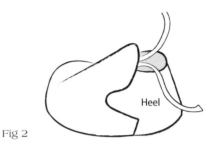

Fig 2

9 Pin the heel piece to the toe piece where they overlap. With two strands of yellow embroidery cotton, work running stitch, with the first four stitches going through both layers to hold this overlap together. Continue the running stitch around the back in between the layers, concealing the stitches. Work the last four stitches through both layers again. Knot the cotton off. Tie the ribbon to finish. Repeat steps 7–9 to assemble the other bootie.

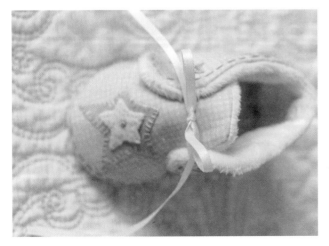

Welcome Bunting

This bunting makes a lovely decoration for the nursery. It has seven flags but you could make more. I used a pompom trim to string the bunting together but ribbon would be pretty too.

You will need...

- Three yellow print fabrics ⅜yd (30cm) each
- Pink or blue fabrics for appliqué (hearts, flowers or stars) 6in x 6in (15.2cm x 15.2cm)
- Three yellow wool felts for appliqué 5in x 5in (12.7cm x 12.7cm) each
- Fusible interfacing 1yd (1m)
- Fusible web and freezer paper
- Ric-rac braid for trim ⅞in x 4½yd (2.1cm x 4.25m)
- Ribbon for hanging tabs ⅛in x 1yd (3mm x 1m)
- Pompom trim or ribbon 4yd (3.75m)
- DMC embroidery cotton (floss) in 3852 yellow and blanc (white), plus colours to match appliqué fabrics

For boy bunting:
- Tan wool felt for rocking horse appliqué 10in x 10in (25.4cm x 25.4cm)
- Oatmeal wool felt for rocking horse appliqué 8in x 8in (20.3cm x 20.3cm)
- DMC embroidery cotton (floss) 310 black, 813 blue and 3821 light yellow

For girl bunting:
- Three green fabrics for leaf appliqués 6in x 6in (15.2cm x 15.2cm)
- DMC embroidery cotton (floss) for flowers 152 pink, 470 green and 3821 light yellow

Finished size:
One triangle is 7½in (19cm) tall x 7in (17.8cm) wide

Directions

1 See the Template section at the back of the book for the relevant templates. From three yellow fabrics cut out fourteen triangular bunting shapes following the cutting line on the template. Set seven aside for backing. Cut interfacing for seven shapes following the sewing (solid) line. Press on to the back of each fabric shape. Trace the embroidery lines on to the bunting.

2 Work the appliqué on the bunting as follows. Trace the large stars, flowers or hearts on to fusible web. Press on to the back of the fabrics and cut out. Trace three leaves for each flower on to the back of fusible web and cut out. Trace small stars, flowers or hearts on to freezer paper. Press on to wool felt and cut out. Trace circle dots on to fusible web, press on to the back of the fabrics and then cut out.

3 Fuse the stars or hearts in place. Pin or glue the wool felt stars or hearts in place. Press the flowers in place with three leaves stuck under each one. Glue or pin the flower centres into place. Fuse a dot in the centre of each motif. Whipstitch in place with one strand of matching embroidery cotton.

4 Work the rocking horse appliqué as follows. Using the templates trace the rocking horse, rocker, tail and mane pieces on to freezer paper. Press the horse shape on to tan wool felt and cut out three. Press the other designs on to oatmeal wool felt and cut out three of each. Glue or pin the horse on to the bunting, noting where the design pieces overlap. Trace three saddles on to fusible web. Press these on to the back of the blue print and cut out. Press into place on the horse. Whipstitch in place with one strand of matching embroidery cotton.

5 Work the embroidery around the edges of the bunting triangles as described in the panel.

6 Tack (baste) ric-rac in place all around the bunting, at the back. Let the ends taper off at the top where they meet. Do not pull the ric-rac or it will cause the piece to curl and not hang flat. Cut two 3in (7.6cm) lengths of narrow ribbon as little hanging tabs for each bunting shape. Fold the ribbon in half, place at the top about 3in (7.6cm) apart and pin or tack in place.

7 Back each bunting triangle by pinning the backing piece right sides together with the front piece. Sew all around leaving an opening on a straight edge for turning through to the right side. Trim, turn through and slipstitch the opening closed. To finish, use the pompom trim or ribbon to hang the bunting.

Embroidery

- Using two strands of yellow embroidery cotton work running stitch following the scallop shape all around. Using three strands of white work French knot dots at the point of each scallop (1).
- For the girl bunting, work the flowers in two strands of pink cotton and lazy daisy stitch for the petals and French knots in light yellow for the centres. Use green cotton and lazy daisy for the leaves (1).
- For the boy bunting, work the stars with two strands of blue and straight stitch. In places I omitted the stitched flower or star where the appliqué overlaps into the scallop (2).
- For the boy bunting, work the embroidery on the rocking horse in backstitch with three strands of light yellow for reins, a straight stitch star on the saddle in yellow, a French knot in black for the eye and dots on the rocker and reins in blue (3).

Newborn Delights

Once the baby has arrived home there are many delights in store, and this chapter shows some practical and yet beautiful projects to help take care of the little one. A small pillow to hang on the bedroom door has an appliquéd sun on one side and a moon on the other to tell the family when the baby is asleep. A handy armchair caddy will be a blessing to a new mum, with its various pockets to store some of the baby's necessities.

A Moses basket is a popular way of keeping the baby close in the early weeks and making a liner and light blanket is a wonderful way to personalize the basket.

Colours in this chapter are a delicate pistachio green, perfect for creating a warm and comforting feeling in the nursery. There are some pretty appliqué motifs on these lovely projects in soft wool felt colours, including hearts, stars and storks, plus tiny embroidered flowers.

3 hour project

Sun and Moon Door Hanger

*This sweet little door sign is perfect for reminding the family that the baby is asleep –
simply turn the sign to the moon and stars side. Ric-rac braid makes an attractive edging.*

You will need...

- Light green print fabric 6in x 12in (15.2cm x 30.5cm)
- Light yellow wool felt for sun centre and moon 6in x 4in (15.2cm x 10.2cm)
- Yellow wool felt for sun 3in x 3in (7.6cm x 7.6cm)
- Light blue wool felt for stars 3in x 3in (7.6cm x 7.6cm)
- Freezer paper
- Light quilt wadding (batting) 6in x 12in (15.2cm x 30.5cm)
- White ribbon ½in (1.3cm) wide x 24in (61cm)
- Light green ric-rac braid ⅞in (2.2cm) wide x 24in (61cm)
- Toy stuffing (fibrefill)
- DMC stranded cotton (floss) 581 green, 3821 yellow, 3761 blue and blanc (white), plus colours to match wool felt colours

Finished size:
5in x 5in (12.7cm x 12.7cm)

➤➤ Directions

1 Cut two backing pieces from green fabric each 5½in x 5½in (14cm x 14cm). See the Template section at the back of the book for the relevant templates. Trace the embroidery lines on to the backing pieces. Back both backing pieces with pieces of wadding (batting) the same size.

2 Work the appliqué by first tracing the moon, star, sun outside and sun inside on to the paper side of the freezer paper. Press the shiny side of the freezer paper on to its corresponding wool felt colour. Cut out the shapes and glue or pin in place. Whipstitch the wool felt appliqués in place with one strand of matching embroidery cotton.

3 Work the embroidery on the project as described in the panel opposite.

›› Embroidery

- Work running stitch with two strands of green embroidery cotton along the outside edge of both pieces. Work scattered French knots with three strands of blanc (1).
- Use two strands of yellow to work running stitch around the inside of the moon. Use three strands of blue for French knot dots at the points of the stars (2).
- Use two strands of yellow and running stitch around the centre of sun. Use three strands of yellow to work French knots on the sun ray points (3).

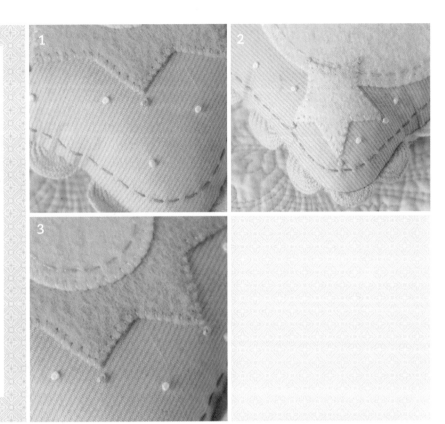

4 Following the template, trim the corners of the backings to a rounded shape – the cutting line is shown as a dashed line and sewing line as a solid line. Tack ric-rac braid to the edge of the backing. Cut two lengths of ribbon each 12in (30.5cm) and pin in place on the ric-rac side.

5 With right sides together, pin the backings together. Sew all around, keeping the ribbon free and leaving an opening for turning. Trim but do not trim the ribbon as this may cause it to fray and come out of the seam. Turn through to the right side, press and stuff. Whipstitch the opening closed to finish.

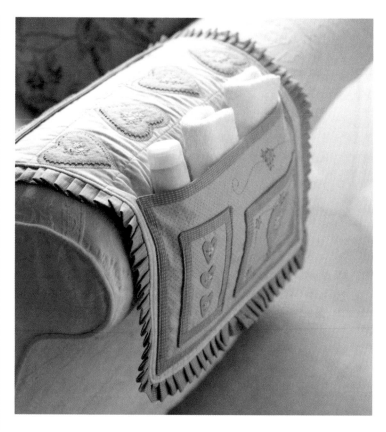

Cosy Chair Caddy

Appliqué hearts and embroidered flowers decorate this handy caddy. It has four different-sized pockets, ideal for storing baby necessities. Pocket B is the perfect size for a baby's bottle.

You will need...

- Off-white print fabric for top ½yd (50cm)
- Light green print fabric for pocket centres ⅓yd (30cm)
- Contrast green fabric for pocket borders, lining and heart appliqué ½yd (50cm)
- Contrast green fabric for pleated trim ⅓yd (30cm)
- Green fabric for backing ½yd (50cm)
- Pink wool felt for heart appliqués 12in x 12in (30.5cm x 30.5cm)
- Fusible web and freezer paper
- Medium-weight fusible interfacing ¾yd (75cm)
- Light quilt wadding (batting) 17in x 25in (43.2cm x 63.5cm)
- DMC embroidery cotton (floss) 581 green, 3821 yellow, 224 pink, 3861 lavender and ecru, plus colours to match wool felt and fabric appliqué

Finished size:
24in x 16in (61cm x 40.6cm)

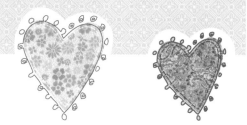

›› Directions

1 See the Template section at the back of the book for the relevant templates. The caddy layout is shown in Fig 1 opposite. Cut one top from off-white fabric 15½in x 23½in (39.4cm x 60cm). Use the template provided to cut rounded corners. Mark the centre points on all sides. Back this piece with light quilt wadding (batting). Set aside for now.

2 Make the pockets as follows. From light green print fabric, cut Pocket A centre 13½in x 8in (34.3cm x 20.3cm). Cut Pocket B centre 3in x 5¼in (7.6cm x 13.3cm). Cut Pocket C centre 6½in x 4¼in (16.5cm x 10.8cm). Cut Pocket D centre 13½in x 5¾in (34.3cm x 14.6cm).

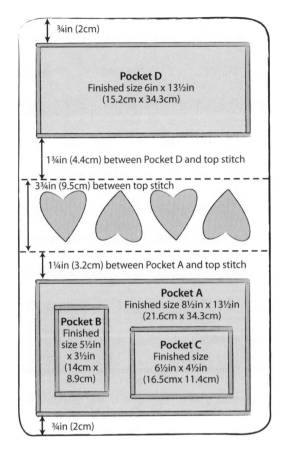

¾in (2cm)

Pocket D
Finished size 6in x 13½in
(15.2cm x 34.3cm)

1¾in (4.4cm) between Pocket D and top stitch

3¾in (9.5cm) between top stitch

1¼in (3.2cm) between Pocket A and top stitch

Pocket A
Finished size 8½in x 13½in
(21.6cm x 34.3cm)

Pocket B
Finished size 5½in x 3½in
(14cm x 8.9cm)

Pocket C
Finished size 6½in x 4½in
(16.5cmx 11.4cm)

¾in (2cm)

Fig 1

3 Cut and sew borders to all the pockets using green contrast fabric. Cut the following pieces of fabric.

Pocket A: two strips for the sides, each 1in x 8in (2.5cm x 20.3cm) and two strips for the top and bottom each 1in x 14½in (2.5cm x 36.8cm).

Pocket B: two strips for the sides, each 1in x 5¼in (2.5cm x 13.3cm) and two strips for the top and bottom, each 1in x 4in (2.5cm x 10.2cm).

Pocket C: two strips for the sides, each 1in x 4¼in (2.5cm x 10.8cm) and two strips for the top and bottom, each 1in x 7½in (2.5cm x 19cm).

Pocket D: two strips for the sides, each 1in x 5¾in (2.5cm x 145.6cm) and two strips for the top and bottom, each 1in x 14½in (2.5cm x 36.8cm).

Using ¼in (6mm) seams sew on the sides and press open. Sew on the top and bottom and press open.

4 Trace the embroidery design on to each of the pockets. Back the pockets with fusible interfacing cut ¼in (6mm) smaller than the finished pocket size and fuse in place with a ¼in (6mm) free edge on all sides to allow for seams.

5 To make the fabric appliqué, trace four large hearts for the centre design on to fusible web. Press the web on to the wrong side of the green fabric. Cut out the shapes on the design line given. Fuse in place as noted on the template. Whipstitch the fabric appliqués in place using one strand of matching cotton.

6 To make the wool felt appliqué, trace three medium hearts and one small heart on to the paper side of the freezer paper. Press the shiny side on to the pink wool felt. Cut out the hearts. Use this freezer paper template to cut out eight medium hearts and three small hearts. Glue or pin in place and then whipstitch the appliqués in place with one strand of matching cotton. Mark the embroidery design on the wool felt hearts. With chalk, pencil or a wash-away marker, make a dot where each flower should go.

7 Work the embroidery on the project as described in the panel below.

8 Cut a backing for each pocket from green print fabric. With right sides together sew all around leaving an opening for turning. Trim seams and clip corners. Turn through, press and then hand stitch the opening closed.

9 Pin pockets B and C to pocket A (see Fig 1). Sew the sides and bottom, leaving the top free, using a topstitch on your sewing machine. Pin the completed pocket ABC set and pocket D in place on your top. Sew in place, through all layers, using a topstitch along the sides and bottom and leaving the top free.

›› Embroidery

- Using embroidery cotton in pink work five lazy daisy stitches about ¼in (6mm) long from the dot marked. Make each one slightly different to give more personality. Lazy daisy stitch a few leaves from each flower and finish with a French knot in yellow in the centre (1).
- Using three strands of ecru embroidery cotton, work lazy daisy petals for all flowers on the wool felt hearts. Use pink lazy daisy for the petals on all the flowers on the pocket tops. Use three strands of cotton for yellow French knot centres. Use two strands of cotton for all green lazy daisy leaves (2).
- Use two strands of cotton in lavender for all running stitches on the pockets. Outline all medium-sized hearts with French knots using three strands of pink (2).

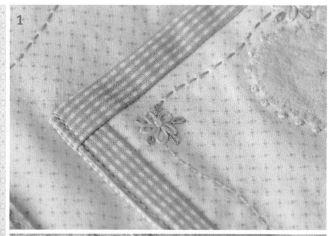

10 To create the pleated trim cut four strips from contrast green fabric, each 2½in x 37in (6.3cm x 94cm). Sew right sides together along all 2½in (6.3cm) edges, creating a large circle, being careful not to let these twist. Press wrong sides together along the length, matching raw edges evenly. Pin in place on the caddy top, matching the raw edge of the top to the raw edge of the trim (with the folded edge of the trim towards the pockets). There is about 30in (76cm)

of trim from corner to corner on the short sides and 43in (109cm) of trim from corner to corner on the long sides. Pin at the centre points marked in the middle of the trim, 15in (38.1cm) from corner to middle on the short sides, and 21½in (54.6cm) from corner to middle on the long sides. Continue pinning the centre of the trim to the centre between pins placed. Tack (baste) pleats in place by folding about ¼in (6mm) of trim every ½in (1.3cm).

11 Cut a piece of backing fabric 17in x 25in (43.2cm x 63.5cm). With right sides together, sew the backing to the caddy front, leaving an opening on a straight edge for turning. Trim, turn through and press. Hand stitch the opening closed. Topstitch ¼in (6mm) in from the edge across the caddy above and below the centre area of four hearts to finish.

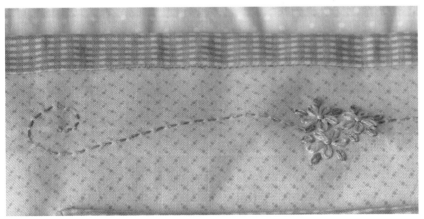

1 week project

Stork Moses Basket

You will need...

For the basket liner:

- Light green print fabric 1½yd (1.5m)
- Contrast light green fabric ¾yd (75cm)
- Antique white, white, peach and yellow wool felt for appliqué 8in x 8in (20.3cm x 20.3cm) each
- Pink wool felt for heart appliqués 12in x 12in (30.5cm x 30.5cm)
- Freezer paper
- Light quilt wadding (batting) ¾yd (75cm)
- White ribbon ¼in (6mm) wide x 80in (203cm)
- DMC embroidery cotton (floss) 581 green, 3852 yellow, 310 black and blanc (white), plus colours to match wool felt colours

For the blanket:

- Light green fabric for blanket top ¾yd (75cm)
- Light green flannel for back ¾yd (75cm)
- Contrast green fabric for pleated trim ⅓yd (30cm)
- Antique white, white, pink, peach and yellow wool felt for appliqués 5in x 5in (12.7cm x 12.7cm) each
- Light wadding (batting) 22in x 28in (56cm x 71cm)
- Freezer paper

- DMC embroidery cotton 581 green, 3852 yellow, 310 black and blanc (white), plus colours to match wool felt colours
- Foam for pad (optional)
- Fabric for pad cover 1yd (1m) (optional)

Finished size:

Liner: 10in x 27in (25.4cm x 68.8cm) with a 3in (7.6cm) deep scallop fold

Blanket: 22in x 28in (55.9cm x 71.1cm)

Many babies spend their early weeks in a Moses basket and sewing a liner and blanket would make a lovely gift for proud new parents. You could also make a cover for the foam pad in the basket. My basket dimensions were 10in x 26in (25.4cm x 66cm) bottom inside, 6in (15.2cm) tall at foot end, 9in (23cm) tall at head end. If your basket is a different size see Tip opposite.

>> Directions for the Liner

1 See the Template section at the back of the book for the relevant templates. Templates 1 and 2 are used together to create a quarter of the bottom shape – see Fig 1. Use the combined templates to cut one bottom piece from green print fabric on the solid line. Flip the combined template to create a bottom 27in (69cm) long x 10½in (26.7cm) wide with rounded edges. Mark the centre points of the head, the foot and the middle. Set this piece aside for now.

2 Cut two sides from print fabric and two sides from contrast fabric using the dimensions given in Fig 2. With right sides together, sew the print sides together along the 10in (25.4cm) and 7in (17.8cm) angled sides to create a circle. Back the contrast sides with wadding (batting) to create a soft edge to your basket. Trim the wadding to the exact size of your contrast pieces. Tack wadding to the wrong side of the contrast pieces. With right sides together sew the contrast sides, catching the wadding in the seam to create another circle. Set these pieces aside for now.

Fig 1 Basket base shape

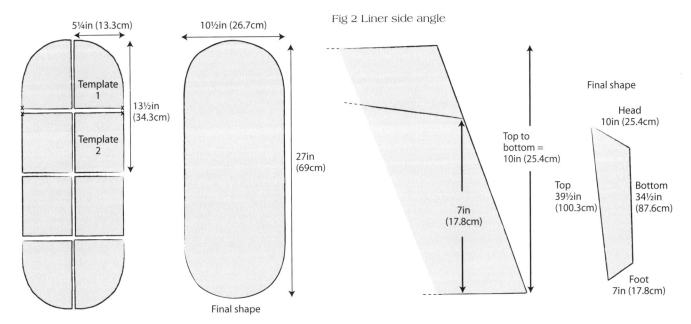

Fig 2 Liner side angle

Final shape

5¼in (13.3cm)

10½in (26.7cm)

Template 1

Template 2

13½in (34.3cm)

27in (69cm)

Final shape

Top to bottom = 10in (25.4cm)

7in (17.8cm)

Head 10in (25.4cm)

Top 39½in (100.3cm)

Bottom 34½in (87.6cm)

Foot 7in (17.8cm)

> **>> TIP**
>
> *If your basket dimensions differ from mine you can adjust the measurements in the following ways. Use the rounded bottom template to add or subtract measurements. Make the bottom shorter by subtracting at the centre line of the template. Subtract width on the straight edges. Take off or add to the sides and scallop in 3in (7.6cm) increments to keep the scallop design. Ease fabric excess to the bottom and scallop, with the tucks evenly dispersed. The foot or head end can be taller if necessary. This may add or subtract length on the sides and bottom. Ease extra fabric to the bottom and scallop as before.*

3 To create the scalloped edges start by cutting four
3½in x 9½in (8.9cm x 24.1cm) pieces and four
3½in x 30½in (8.9cm x 77.5cm) pieces. Set two of each
of these lengths aside for backing. Trace the scallop edge
(the dashed line on the appliqué template) on to the
pieces (see Tip below). There are three scallops on a
9½in (24.1cm) length and ten scallops on a 30½in
(77.5cm) length. Trace the embroidery design on to the
scallops. Back the pieces with wadding.

›› TIP

*To avoid lots of tracing make the scallop template with freezer paper.
Trace the scallop on to the paper side of the freezer paper and trim
on the traced line. Press on to the fabric lengths, marking the scallop
cutting line. Gently pull up the freezer paper, move it up ¼in (6mm),
press again and mark the sewing line. You can use this template to
mark the cutting line, sewing line and embroidery running stitch line.*

›› Embroidery

- Using two strands of embroidery cotton, work running stitch in green along the liner scallops. Work French knot dots on the scallops in blanc (white) (1).
- Using black cotton work French knot eyes on the baby and the stork. Use yellow cotton to backstitch the stork legs (2).
- On the blanket use three strands of blanc (white) to work a lazy daisy bow at the top of the stork beak (2).

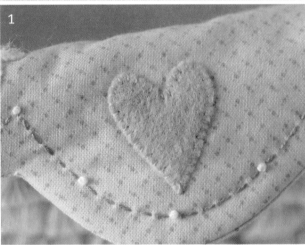

4 Work the appliqué by tracing the stork, baby head, blanket and heart on to the paper side of the freezer paper. Press the shiny side on to the corresponding wool felt colours and cut out the shapes. Cut six storks with baby motifs and twenty hearts. Glue or pin all in place following the photographs. There is a stork and baby in the middle scallop of each short-length scallop. In the long-length scallop the hearts and stork pattern is: two hearts, a stork set, four hearts, a stork set and two hearts. Whipstitch the wool felt appliqués in place with one strand of matching embroidery cotton.

5 Work the embroidery as described in the panel, left. The liner and blanket both have embroidery. Then trim the scalloped edge ¼in (6mm) from the solid line (the dashed line given on the template).

6 Cut eight lengths of ribbon each 10in (25.4cm) long. Pin the ribbon to the edge 1½in (3.8cm) down on all straight edges of the sides and allowing ½in (1.3cm) to extend out into the seam for strength. With right sides together, place the corresponding backs on to your trimmed scallop edge. Being careful not to catch ribbon in the seams, sew down the sides and along the scallop on the solid line. Trim but do not trim the ribbon as it may fray out of the seam. Clip to the points, turn and press. Trim the top of the scallop so both edges and wadding are even.

7 With right sides together, pin the scallop pieces to the contrast sides (the sides with the wadding). Centre the long scallops around the foot side and head side, matching seams to the middle of the scallop. Pin all around. Fit the short scallops to the spaces left between. There should be approximately ½in (1.3cm) between both sides of the short scallop and long scallop. Make sure all are even, easing any excess scallop or sides into the seam evenly. Tack (baste) all around. Pin the print fabric sides to the prepared contrast, with the scallops right sides together. Tack and then sew all round. Trim, turn and press. Make sure all bottom edges of the sides are even, trimming if necessary.

8 Pin the sides to the bottom, matching the points of the middle bottom to the middle of the sides. The seams for the head and foot should match the centre of the rounded head and foot. Pin, easing in any extra fabric. Tack and sew all around (a few tucks may occur). Carefully trim and then zigzag stitch the edge to finish.

9 If you have made a pad with foam or your basket came with one, you could cover this pad with fabric. Just trace your pad over two layers of fabric and add ¾in (2cm) all around. Sew a ¼in (6mm) seam leaving a large opening for turning. Turn through, place the pad inside and close with a whipstitch.

›› Directions for the Blanket

1 Cut a top piece 20½in x 26½in (52cm x 67.3cm). Round the corners using the blanket template given in the Template section at the back of the book. Mark the middle points of all sides. Trace the embroidery lines on to the blanket top and then back with wadding (batting).

2 Following the freezer paper and cutting instructions in step 4 of the liner, cut two stork sets and six hearts. Glue or pin the appliqués in place and whipstitch with one strand of matching embroidery cotton.

3 Embroider following the directions in the embroidery panel. Trim the blanket top and wadding even.

4 To create the pleated edge trim, cut four strips of contrast fabric each 2½in x 44in (6.3cm x 111.7cm). Sew the short ends right sides together to create one large 174in (442cm) diameter circle. Fold in half wrong sides together along the length so it is 1¼in (3.2cm) wide. Press well and make sure the edges are even. Pin the raw edge of the trim to the edge of the blanket top, starting with a short (20½in/52cm) side. Pin at the centre of a corner, measure approximately 37in (94cm) of trim and pin to the corner. Measure 50in (127cm) of trim (on the long 26½in/67.3cm side), repeat 37in and then 50in. I continued pinning until there was a pin about every 3in (7.6cm), with 5in (12.7cm) of trim between.

5 With a long length of thread tack ¼in (6mm) pleats in the trim every ½in (1.3cm) or so. There's no need to be perfect, just ease each pleat in, making sure you use up all excess trim before reaching the next pin.

6 Cut a backing piece 22in x 28in (55.9cm x 71.1cm). With right sides together sew the back to the front, leaving an opening on a straight edge for turning. Trim, turn through and press. Slipstitch the opening closed. Topstitch all around through all layers to finish.

Baby Girl

The projects in this chapter are filled with beautiful flowers, perfect to celebrate the arrival of a baby girl. Stuffed flower-shaped decorations are really easy to make and are great as quick gifts to adorn a cot or pram (stroller). A useful carry-all that hangs neatly on a wall has eight pockets in different sizes and makes a practical addition to the nursery. A delightful cot quilt in sugary pinks and yellows is filled with pretty appliqué flowers, framed by appliqué and patchwork blocks. Ric-rac braid makes an attractive addition and the cot quilt uses a wide-width trim to great effect.

Pink is the main colour in this chapter, of course, in all its many girly shades, with added touches of lilac, lemon, green and blue for contrast. Cotton prints and wool felt are used for easy patchwork and appliqué, with satin bows and embroidery stitches for further details.

Flower Decorations

These sweet little decorations are perfect to adorn a cot or pram (stroller). They can be made in any size you like simply by enlarging or reducing the template size.

You will need...

- Print fabric 8in x 16in (20.3cm x 40.6cm)
- Pink wool felt 6in x 6in (15.2cm x 15.2cm)
- Two green fabrics for leaves each 5in x 3in (12.7cm x 7.6cm)
- Pink fabric for centre dot 3in x 3in (7.6cm x 7.6cm)
- Fusible web
- Lightweight quilt wadding (batting) 7in x 7in (17.8cm x 17.8cm)
- Ribbon ⅝in (1.6cm) wide x 10in (25.4cm)
- Velcro tape ½in (1.3cm) wide x 5in (12.7cm)
- Fabric glue
- Toy stuffing (fibrefill)
- Embroidery stranded cotton (floss) to match dot fabric and wool felt

Finished size:
4½in (11.4cm) diameter

>> Directions

1 Using the templates given in the Template section at the back of the book, cut two large flowers from print fabric ¼in (6mm) larger than the finished design (one for the front and one for a backing). Cut one medium flower from wool felt. Trace a circle for the flower centre on to fusible web, iron on to the back of the pink fabric and cut out.

2 Cut two leaves from each of the green fabrics ¼in (6mm) larger than the size given in the template. With right sides together, sew around each leaf, leaving about ¾in (2cm) open at the base. Trim around the leaf to leave ⅛in (3mm), turn through and press.

3 Layer the leaves and flowers in this order: large flower, wool felt flower and circle. Position the leaves under the wool felt flower and pin in place. Trim away leaf excess. Glue or pin the wool felt flower in place. Fuse the circle to the wool felt flower by pressing.

4 Back the flower with light quilt wadding and tack (baste) to hold. With one strand of stranded cotton, whipstitch the wool felt flower, catching the leaves in the stitching to hold. Whipstitch the circle in place.

5 Pin the leaves back temporarily to keep them out of your seam. With right sides together, sew the backing to the flower all around, through all layers. Trim and clip the points where the flower petals seams pivot. Make a 2in (5cm) slash in the back of your flower, turn through and press. Stuff lightly and then whipstitch this slash closed.

6 Fold ½in (1.3cm) of ribbon down on one side for a hem. Cut the Velcro into 2in (5cm) lengths. Sew or glue one side of the Velcro (the hooked side or looped side) to this end. Flip the ribbon over. Repeat this step for the opposite end of the ribbon. The Velcro should be at each end and on opposite sides. Centre the ribbon to the back of the flower covering up your previous seam. Hand stitch the ribbon over this seam. Attach to the sides of a cot or pram (stroller).

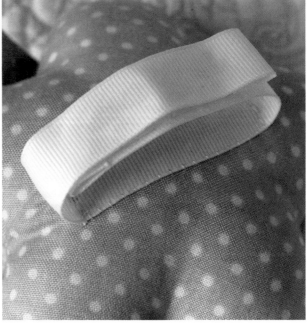

Floral Wall Tidy

This delightful carry-all hanging has eight pockets in varying sizes and would make a useful present for a mum-to-be. The colours and motifs are easily changed to suit a little boy.

You will need...

- Off-white fabric for centre background ¾yd (75cm)

- Pink fabric for border, tabs and backing 1¼yd (1.25m)

- Two pink print fabrics for pockets and flowers ¼yd (25cm) each

- Two pink fabrics for basket pockets and flowers ½yd (50cm) each

- Yellow fabric for pockets and flower ⅓yd (30cm)

- Two purple, two blue and three green fabrics for appliqués ¼yd (25cm) each

- Three pink wool felts for flowers 18in x 18in (45.7cm x 45.7cm) each

- Fusible web and freezer paper

- Light wadding (batting) for backing 27in x 46in (68.6cm x 116.8cm) and for pocket backing 36in x 36in (91.4cm x 91.4cm)

- Pink satin ribbon ⅜in (1cm) wide x 20in (50.8cm)

- A hanger

- DMC embroidery cotton (floss) 224 light pink and 3859 dark pink, plus colours to match fabrics and felts

Finished size:
24in x 42in (61cm x 106.7cm) with tabs

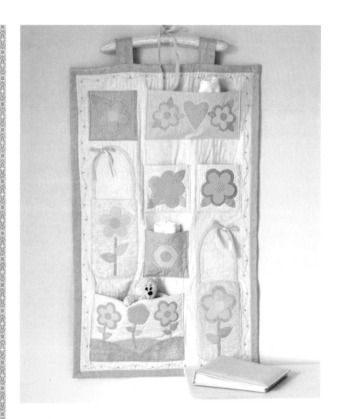

›› Directions

1 See the Template section at the back of the book for the relevant templates. The tidy has four different pockets, some of which are made more than once in different fabrics – refer to Fig 1 for the layout and pockets. Start by cutting the centre background from off-white fabric 22½in x 37½in (57.1cm x 95.2cm). Border this piece by cutting two strips of pink fabric each 1½in x 37½in (3.8cm x 95.2cm), sew them to the sides of the centre piece and press open. Cut two strips each 1½in x 24½in (3.8cm x 62.2cm) and sew to the top and bottom of the centre piece and press open.

2 Trace the embroidery lines from the relevant template on to the outer edge of the central cream piece. Back this completed piece with wadding (batting). Work the embroidery as described in the panel opposite.

3 Cut the following pieces of fabric for the pockets (see Fig 1).

Single flower pockets: cut four pockets, three in pink, one in yellow, each 6½in (16.5cm) square. Cut the same sizes again for the pocket backs.

Flower and heart pocket: cut one pink piece 6½in x 12½in (16.5cm x 31.7cm). Cut a second piece for the pocket back.

Flower scene pocket: cut one yellow piece 9½in x 12½in (24.1cm x 31.7cm). Cut a second piece for the pocket back.

Flower basket pockets: to make the bias handles for the baskets, cut two 17in (43.2cm) squares from pink fabric. Cut two rectangles from pink to match your bias handles 6½in x 10½in (16.5cm x 26.7cm). Cut two more rectangles for the pocket backs. Following the guide on the template, round the rectangle corners.

Fig 1 wall tidy layout

>> Embroidery

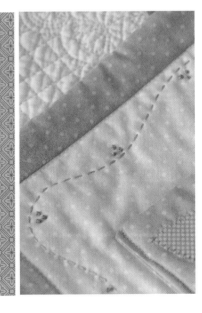

- Using three strands of light pink embroidery cotton, work running stitch in a gently wavy line all around the edge of the cream panel.
- With three strands of dark pink cotton work French knot dot clusters at each curve. Set the piece aside for now.

4 Flower basket pockets: to make the bias handles for the baskets, take the 17in (43.2cm) square and from corner to opposite corner, cut a strip 1in (2.5cm) wide on the diagonal. Press under ¼in (6mm) along each long edge to the back. Save your leftover triangles for flower appliqués.

>> TIP
I backed my pockets with lightweight quilt wadding (batting) and appliquéd all flower layers through the wadding for a 'quilted' effect. But before sewing the pocket backs, I trimmed the wadding ¼in (6mm) away from the edges all around so the corners of the pockets would be pointed and crisp.

5 The green 'land' pieces for the flower scene pocket are a total size of 9½in x 12½in (24.1cm x 31.7cm). Trace the land pieces on to fusible web and press on to the back of the green fabrics. Cut out the pieces ¼in (6mm) larger in order to fit beneath each other and to get caught into the seam (shown on the template by dashed lines). Whipstitch these pieces in place on the yellow rectangle of fabric with one strand of matching embroidery cotton.

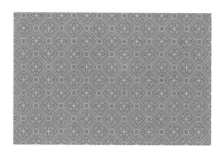

6 For the flower appliqués on the wall tidy use the relevant templates from the back of the book. The large flowers are used for the tall flower basket pocket and the square single pockets. Trace the large and small flower outsides, stems, leaves, centre dots and large heart from the templates on to fusible web. Press on to your fabrics and cut out. Trace the middle flowers on to the paper side of freezer paper and cut out. Following the template, and overlapping where necessary, position the pieces. Press fused pieces and glue or pin wool felts in place. Back each pocket with light wadding. With one strand of matching embroidery cotton, whipstitch the appliqués in place.

>> TIP
The flowers and stars appliqués can be used in all of the baby girl and baby boy projects, including the cot bumper, nappy stacker and pillow.

7 With right sides together, back each pocket with its corresponding backing piece. Sew all around, leaving an opening for turning. Trim corners and excess fabrics from the seam, turn through and press. Slipstitch the openings closed.

8 Place and pin all pockets on to the centre panel following the layout in Fig 1. Pin the bias handles in place at each end under the top of the flower basket pockets. Pulling the pocket top back on the basket pockets, topstitch the handles in place ⅛in (3mm) away from both sides. Now topstitch all pockets on the sides and bottom. I reverse stitched ¼in (6mm) at the tops for extra strength.

9 Make the tabs for the wall tidy by cutting two tabs from pink fabric 4½in x 8in (11.4cm x 20.3cm). Fold a tab in half, right sides together along the length. Sew a ¼in (6mm) seam, turn through and press with the seam in the middle. Fold the tab in half with the seam inside. Make the second tab in the same way. Pin the tabs in place on the top of the wall tidy, 8in (20.3cm) apart at the middle and about 6¼in (15.9cm) from each edge, with the tabs pointing inwards.

10 Pin the backing fabric piece to the completed front, right sides together. Sew all around leaving an opening at the bottom for turning through. I double stitched at the tabs for strength. Clip corners, trim seams, turn through to the right side and press. Slipstitch the opening closed. Topstitch through all layers where the border meets the centre backing. To finish, cut the length of satin ribbon in two, tie each piece into a bow and hand tack (baste) in place on the basket handles.

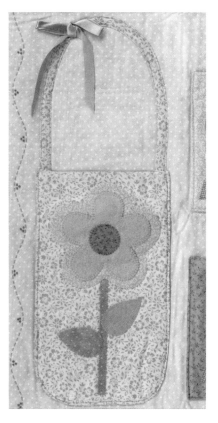

Flower Cot Quilt

This gorgeous cot quilt filled with pretty flowers has a centre panel framed by alternating appliqué blocks and square-in-a-square blocks. A soft minkee fabric backs the quilt.

You will need...

- Off-white fabric for centre and block centres 1yd (1m)
- Four pink print and four yellow print fabrics for blocks ¼yd (25cm) each
- Yellow fabric for border ⅓yd (30cm)
- Three green fabrics for land, leaf and stem appliqués ½yd (50cm) each
- Three pinks, two blues and two lavender fabrics for flower appliqués ¼yd (25cm) each
- Two pink fabrics for dot appliqués 8in x 8in (20.3cm x 20.3cm) each
- Three pink wool felts for flowers 18in x 18in (45.7cm x 45.7cm) each
- Large ric-rac braid for border 1½in (3.8cm) x 4yd (3.75m)
- Pink fabric for binding ½yd (50cm)
- Fusible web and freezer paper
- Light quilt wadding (batting) 45in x 54in (114.3cm x 137.2cm)
- Backing fabric (or minkee – see Tip, right) 45in x 54in (114.3cm x 137.2cm)
- DMC embroidery cotton (floss) 224 light pink and 3859 dark pink, plus colours to match fabrics and felts

Finished size:
41in x 49in (104cm x 124.5cm)

>> Directions

1 See the Template section at the back of the book for the relevant templates. The centre panel appliqué is made up of eight parts. Cut the centre from off-white fabric 20½in x 28½in (52cm x 72.4cm). For the land pieces, use the templates to trace the pieces on to fusible web (see Fig 1 for the layout of the centre panel). Press on to the back of the green fabrics. Cut out ¼in (6mm)

> ## >> TIP
> *I used minkee for a backing, which is a knitted fabric. You will need to back this with interfacing to stabilize it and prevent stretch. Buy as much medium-weight interfacing to back the minkee as needed depending on the width of interfacing. Follow the manufacturer's instructions for using interfacing.*

larger to allow the pieces to fit beneath each other and get caught into the seam of the first border (shown on the pattern by dashed lines). Trace the embroidery lines on to the land pieces B and C. Press piece A, matching the left edge to the edge of the off-white centre piece. Press piece B overlapping piece A and matching the right edge and bottom. Now add piece C, matching the left edge and bottom and overlapping piece B. Whipstitch these pieces with one strand of matching embroidery cotton.

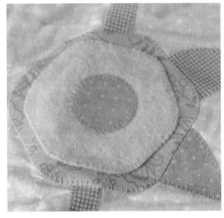

Fig 1 - centre panel appliqué

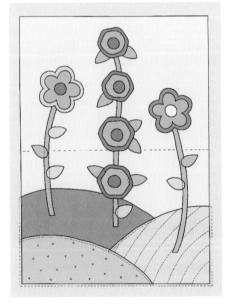

2 To create the first yellow border, cut two side strips each 2½in x 28½in (6.3cm x 72.4cm). Sew these to the sides of the off-white centre piece, catching the land pieces in the seam. Press open. Cut two strips for the top and bottom each 2½in x 24½in (6.3cm x 62.2cm). Sew to the top and bottom of the centre piece, catching the land pieces in the seam. Press open.

3 To work the flower appliqués within the centre panel, trace the large flowers, stems, leaves and circle dots from the templates on to fusible web. Press on to your appliqué fabrics and cut out. Trace the medium size flowers on to the paper side of the freezer paper and cut out. Position the pieces as shown in Fig 1, overlapping where necessary. Press the fused pieces and glue or pin the wool felts into place. With one strand of matching embroidery cotton, whipstitch in place. Set this piece aside for now.

Nine flower blocks are needed for the quilt. Cut nine off-white centres each 5½in x 5½in (14cm x 14cm). Add a border to each square using pink prints, as follows. Cut two side strips each 2in x 5½in (5cm x 14cm). Sew to the sides and press open. Cut two strips for the top and bottom each 2in x 8½in (5cm x 21.6cm). Sew to the top and bottom and press open.

5 To work the flower appliqués on the blocks trace nine large

flowers, nine circle dots and eighteen leaves on to fusible web. Iron the flowers on to the pink, lavender and blue fabrics. Iron the circle dots on to the pink fabrics. Iron the leaves on to green fabrics. Trace one or two medium flowers on to freezer paper (see Tip). Cut out nine pink wool felt flowers from different pinks. Cut out the large flowers, leaves and pink circles. Layer on each flower block in the following order. Press on two leaves (in different positions for each), press a large flower, glue or pin a medium pink wool felt flower and finally press a pink circle to the centre of this flower. With one strand of matching embroidery cotton, whipstitch the appliqués in place.

6 Nine square-in-a-square blocks are needed. Cut nine off-white centres each 2½in x 2½in (6.3cm x 6.3cm). Add a border in pink, cutting

>> TIP

If you trace shapes on to freezer paper once or twice you can reuse each shape at least six times. Trace on the paper side, press on to wool felt, cut out the shape and then peel off. Re-iron shape on to wool felt and cut out, again and again.

two strips for sides each 2in x 2½in (5cm x 6.3cm). Sew to the sides and press open. Cut the top and bottom border strips each 2in x 5½in (5cm x 14cm). Sew to the top and bottom and press open. Add a second border in yellow. Cut two strips for the sides each 2in x 5½in (5cm x 14cm). Sew to the sides and press open. Cut top and bottom strips 2in x 8½in (5cm x 21.6cm). Sew to the top and bottom and press open.

7 Join the blocks together in rows (Fig 2) and sew to the sides of the centre panel and then to the top and bottom.

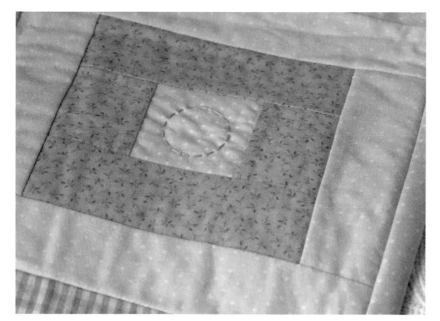

Fig 2

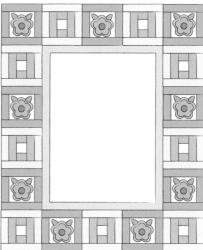

8 Trace the circle shapes in the centre of the square-in-a-square blocks by tracing the circle on to freezer paper. Cut out, press the circle on to the centre off-white section and with your favourite marking pen, trace around the circle. Peel off the freezer paper shape and repeat for the other blocks.

9 Back the quilt top with wadding (batting) and tack (baste) to hold in place – see Backing with Wadding.

10 Pin the ric-rac braid in place on the first yellow border, pivoting at the corners. At the ends, sew a French seam by first sewing wrong sides together. Trim close to the seam and then sew right sides together to finish. Press the seam. With your sewing machine, sew the ric-rac in place following the curve on each side to secure the braid.

11 Work the embroidery on the quilt as described in the panel, right.

12 Tack (baste) your backing fabric to the wrong side of the quilt. Cut binding to your favourite width, I used 3in (7.6cm) binding for this quilt, and bind following the instructions in Binding a Quilt.

>> Embroidery

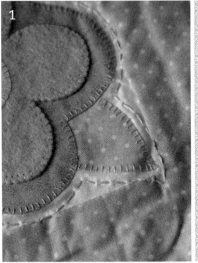

- With three strands of light pink embroidery cotton, stitch a running stitch ¼in (6mm) away from the large flowers. Running stitch the traced dots also in light pink (1).
- Work the dashed line on land piece B in light pink running stitch. Add light pink French knots on the land piece C (2).
- On the ric-rac, work the embroidery using three strands of dark pink cotton for trios of French knots. Use three strands of cotton in lighter pink to work the running stitch (3).

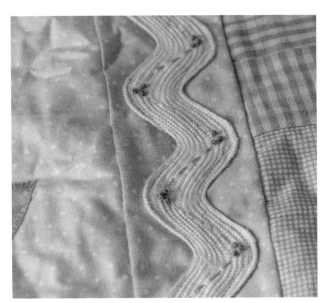

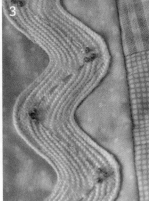

Baby Boy

The adorable projects in this chapter
are perfect to welcome a baby boy into
the world and together make up a set
that will look wonderful in any nursery.
A rocking horse motif has been used as
the centrepiece on a gorgeous cot quilt,
surrounded by a border of appliqué star
blocks. The star appliqués are easy to do
and feature again on a soft cot bumper,
which can be adjusted to fit any cot size.
The rocking horse appears in a smaller
size on a useful nappy stacker and there
is also a small pillow that could be used
decoratively or filled with pot-pourri.

Soft blues, calm creams and warm coffee
colours have been used for these nursery
projects. The fabrics are a mix of cottons
with dainty checks, spots and stripes
and delicately coloured wool felts. The
techniques used are all straightforward,
with simple piecing, quilting and
fusible web appliqué.

3 hour project

Sweet Dreams Pillow

This adorable pillow is easy to make and a great way to use up fabric scraps. The jumbo ric-rac trim adds a decorative touch. The colours and motifs could be changed to suit a little girl.

You will need...

- Blue print fabric for front and back ⅓yd (30cm)
- Yellow print fabric for star appliqué 8in x 8in (20.3cm x 20.3cm)
- Blue wool felt for star appliqué 6in x 6in (15.2cm x 15.2cm)
- Blue print fabric for circle appliqué 3in x 3in (7.6cm x 7.6cm)
- Ric-rac braid 1½in (3.8cm) wide x 1⅓yd (1.3m)
- Fusible web and freezer paper
- Lightweight quilt wadding (batting) 12in x 10in (30.5cm x 25.5cm)
- Toy stuffing (fibrefill) 12oz (340g)
- DMC stranded cotton (floss) 813 blue and in colours to match appliqué

Finished size:
9in x 10in (23cm x 25.5cm)

›› Directions

1 Cut a front and back for the pillow out of the blue print fabric 9½in x 11in (24.1cm x 28cm). Set the back piece aside for now. Back the front piece with a 10in x 12in (25.5cm x 30.5cm) piece of lightweight wadding (batting).

2　See the Template section for the relevant templates. For the appliqué, trace the large star and circle from the template on to the paper side of the fusible web. Back the yellow fabric with the fusible web star and cut out the star. Back the blue fabric with the fusible web circle and cut out the circle. Trace the medium star on to freezer paper. Iron the star on to the blue wool felt and cut out the star. Press to fuse the large star to the middle of the pillow front. Pin or spot glue the medium blue star to the large star. Fuse the blue circle to the middle of both stars. With a single strand of stranded cotton in a colour to match the appliqués, whipstitch the appliqués in place

3　Using three strands of blue stranded cotton, embroider a running stitch all around the large star ¼ in (6mm) away from the edge.

4　To make up the pillow, pin the ric-rac braid to the right side of the pillow front all around the edge, pivoting and pinning at the corners and matching the middle of the ric-rac to the edge of the pillow. (The solid middle of the ric-rac needs to end up in the seam.) Leave one edge unpinned and where the ric-rac ends meet sew a French seam. Do this by first sewing the wrong sides of the trim together and trimming close to the seam. Sew with right sides together and then press. Continue pinning the ric-rac to the final edge of the pillow. Tack (baste) the ric-rac in place.

5　Take the pillow back piece cut earlier and with right sides together, pin it to the pillow front. Sew together all round leaving an opening for turning. Trim the corners to reduce bulk, turn the pillow through to the right side and stuff. Close the opening with whipstitching to finish.

Nappy Stacker

This handy bag is a great way to store nappies (diapers) and looks much nicer than plastic storage. It has a cardboard base, with an easy-access front opening.

You will need...

- Blue fabric for sides, bottom and back 1⅓yd (1.3m)
- Off-white fabric for top and trim ½yd (50cm)
- Two blue fabrics for appliqués 5in x 5in (12.7cm x 12.7cm) each
- Tan wool felt for horse appliqué 9in x 6in (23cm x 15.2cm)
- Oatmeal wool felt for mane, tail and rocker appliqué 8in x 6in (20.3cm x 15.2cm)
- Three yellow wool felts for star appliqués 9in x 9in (23cm x 23cm)
- Yellow fabric for saddle star appliqué 2in x 2in (5cm x 5cm)
- Medium weight fusible interfacing 2¼yd (2.25m)
- Fusible web
- Cardboard for base 8½in x 12½in (21.5cm x 31.7cm)
- One small coat hanger
- DMC stranded cotton (floss) 310 black, 813 blue, 3821 yellow, plus colours to match fabrics and appliqués

Finished size:
12½in wide x 25in high x 8½in deep (31.7cm x 63.5cm x 21.5cm)

›› Directions

1. Start by cutting your fabric pieces. From blue fabric cut two fronts each 16in x 18in (40.5cm x 45.7cm) and one back 13in x 18in (33cm x 45.7cm). Cut two sides each 9in x 18in (23cm x 45.7cm) and one bottom 9in x 13in (23cm x 33cm). Cut two covers

›› TIP

Check to make sure your hanger will fit into the shape for the hanger top. If it needs to be altered, only change the shape of the top – try not to change the width. If the width does need to change, add this extra measurement divided into fronts and back tops only. So, if you add 1in (2.5cm), add ¼in (6mm) to the widths on each front and ½in (1.3cm) to the back top. These pieces will be at a slight angle from top to bottom. I would leave the bottom and side measurements as they are.

for the cardboard 9in x 13in (23cm x 33cm). From off-white fabric cut two top shapes each 10in x 14in (25.5cm x 35.5cm) and two white pieces for trim 2½in x 18in (6.3cm x 45.7cm).

2 Trim your side pieces as follows (see Fig 1). At one short 9in (23cm) edge, measure 2¼in (5.7cm) in from each side and mark. This will leave 4½in (11.4cm) in the centre. With a ruler, trim from the mark to the bottom corner of other short side to create diagonal sides. Repeat on the other side. The sides should now be 4½in (11.4cm) at the top, 9in (23cm) at the bottom and 18in (45.7cm) long.

Fig 1

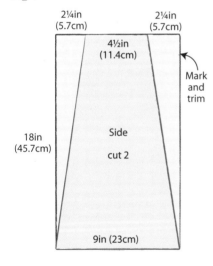

3 Back the following pieces with medium-weight fusible interfacing: two blue fronts, two blue sides, one blue back, one blue bottom and two off-white top shape pieces.

4 Prepare the front pieces by trimming a left and a right front side with the off-white fabric strips. Turn ¼in (6mm) to the wrong side along both side lengths of each trim piece. With wrong sides together, press in half so the trim is 1in x 18in (2.5cm x 45.7cm). Place the 18in (45.7cm) long front piece into the trim piece between the fold. The front piece should fit right up against the fold. Pin in place and then topstitch ⅛in (3mm) from the turned-under edge, catching the top side and under side of the trim in the topstitch. Repeat this process for the other side. With sewing thread, make a running stitch for gathering along the top and bottom of the blue fabric ⅛in (3mm) from the edge, leaving long tails. Do not include the trim in this gathering stitch.

5 Appliqué the stars to the front pieces by first tracing the star on to freezer paper and using this to cut out six stars from yellow wool felts. Trace six blue circles on to the paper side of the fusible web and press to the back of three blue fabrics. Cut out the circles. Pin or glue three wool felt stars to each front piece. Fuse a circle into the middle of each star. Whipstitch the edges of the appliqués with a single strand of matching stranded cotton.

6 Prepare the top shape by tracing the rocking horse, mane, tail and rocker on to freezer paper. The design overlap is indicated by dashed lines. From wool felt, cut out a tan rocking horse and an oatmeal mane, tail and rocker. Trace the saddle, star and the tiny circles on the rocker on to fusible web. Press the saddle and circles to the wrong side of the blue fabric and the star to the wrong side of the yellow fabric. Cut out the shapes. Position all the pieces on one of your off-white top shapes. Pin or glue the wool felts in place. Press the fusible shapes in place. Whipstitch the appliqué edges with a single strand of matching stranded cotton.

7 Embroider the rocking horse as described in the embroidery panel opposite.

8 The nappy holder is now ready to be sewn together, joining the pieces as shown in Fig 2, starting with a left front piece.

Fig 2

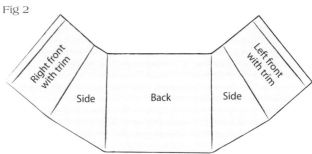

9 Attach the bottom as follows (see Fig 3). On one side of the 13in (33cm) length, mark the middle at 6½in (16.5cm). With right sides together, pin the off-white trim piece at the middle mark. Butt the other trim piece up to this at the middle and pin. Pin the side seams at the corners of the bottom piece and pin the back piece to the other 13in (33cm) side. Pull on the gathering stitch you made earlier to gather up the front pieces so they fit from the side corner to the trim and then pin and tack (baste). Sew all around stopping ¼in (6mm) from each edge, pivoting your needle and turning your work. Check to make sure no excess tucks are caught in your sewing and then finish the seam with a zigzag stitch.

Fig 3

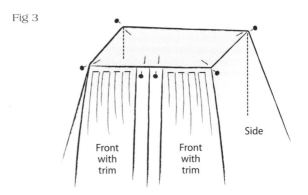

›› Embroidery

- Backstitch the bridle using three strands of yellow stranded cotton.
- Work a French knot on the bridle using three strands of blue cotton.
- Work a French knot for the eye using three strands of black cotton.

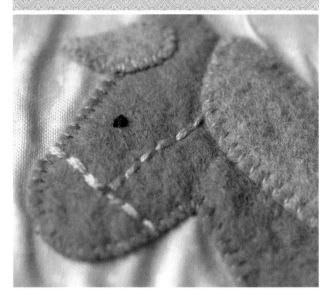

removing the pins one at a time. Sew all around. Check to make sure no excess tucks are caught. Finish the raw edge with a zigzag stitch.

Fig 4A and B

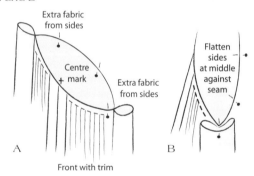

10 Attach the top by sewing the top shape right sides together, leaving an opening at the top for the hanger. Turn right side out and press. Mark the centre of the top shape front, about 6⅜in (16cm) in from the side (Fig 4A and 4B). With right sides together, butt the front trim pieces to this mark. Pin the side seams of the front to the side seams of the top shape. Pull the running stitches to gather the front fabric to fit. Pin the side seams of the back to the side seams of the top shape – this will be right next to the previous pin. The extra fabric from the sides will be loose. Pin at the middle of the loose fabric to the top shape seam. There will be three pins almost on top of each other now. Flatten this loose fabric to fold against the back and front evenly and overlap (this should overlap the gathers too). Pin and tack (baste),

11 Finish the top with a running stitch using three strands of blue stranded cotton. This not only looks cute but also holds down the seam at the opening.

12 For the cardboard base, place the two blue 9in x 13in (23cm x 33cm) pieces right sides together and sew around three sides. Turn right side out and press the un-sewn seam to the inside. Place the cardboard shape inside and with matching sewing thread whipstitch the opening closed. Put this piece into the bottom to create a flat base. Put the hanger through the opening and the stacker is now ready to be filled.

Stars Cot Bumper

This soft bumper features star appliqué squares alternating with quilted motif squares. It could be made longer or shorter to suit your crib size. Colours and motifs could be changed for a girl.

You will need...

- Blue print fabric for front and ties 1½yd (1.5m)
- Off-white print fabric for front 1yd (1m)
- Blue print fabric for backing 1¼yd (1.25m)
- Four yellows prints for star appliqués ¼yd (25cm) each
- Three wool felts in blue for appliqués ¼yd (25cm) each or 12in x 12in (30.5 x 30.5cm) each
- Three blue prints for circle appliqués 6in x 6in (15.2cm x 15.2cm) each
- Light wadding (batting) ¾yd x 90in (75cm x 230cm)
- Lofty quilt wadding ¾yd x 90in (75cm x 230cm)
- Fusible web and freezer paper
- DMC floss 813 blue for embroidery and in colours to match your yellows and blues for appliqué

Finished size:
9in x 164in (23cm x 416.5cm)

❯❯ Directions

1 For the head and foot of the bumper cut six squares 9½in x 9½in (24.1cm x 24.1cm), cutting four from blue print fabric and two from off-white fabric. For the sides of the bumper cut ten rectangles 9½in x 11in (24.1cm x 28cm), cutting four from blue print fabric and six from off-white fabric.

2 See the Template section for the relevant templates. Use the templates to appliqué stars to every off-white square or rectangle. Trace eight large stars and circles on to the paper side of the fusible web. Trace one medium star on to the paper side of the freezer paper. Apply fusible web stars to the back of the four yellow fabrics and fusible web circles to the back of the three blue fabrics. Cut out eight large yellow stars from different colours, cut eight medium stars from blue wool felts and eight blue circles. Fuse yellow stars to the middle of each off-white

Fig 1

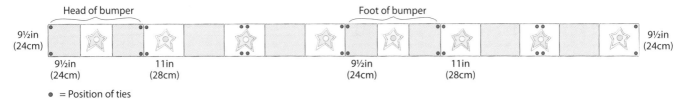

square or rectangle. Pin or spot glue blue wool felt medium stars and fuse blue circles to the centre of each star set. Whipstitch the appliqué edges using one strand of stranded cotton in a matching colour.

3 Sew the front of the bumper by sewing all the squares and rectangles together along the 9½in (24.1cm) edge, following the order in Fig 1. You should have sixteen blocks attached, measuring in total 159½in (405.1cm) long.

4 Back this long piece with lightweight wadding (batting) cut 10in (25.5cm) wide. Piece the wadding together by butting the ends so they lay flat. With one strand of sewing thread, whipstitch the pieces together. Pin, tack (baste) or spray glue your wadding to the back of the bumper to hold it in place.

5 Embroider the appliqués and the star motifs as described in the panel overleaf.

6 Make the ties by cutting twenty-four strips from blue print fabric 2½in x 9½in (6.3cm x 24.1cm). Fold each strip in half lengthwise, wrong sides together, and sew along the side and across one end. Turn each tie right side out and press. Pin the ties in place on the bumper, right sides together and with the raw edge of the tie matching the raw edge of the bumper, in the positions shown by red dots Fig 1. Tack (baste) the ties in place.

7 Cut two pieces of lofty wadding 11in x 90in (28cm x 228.5cm). Whipstitch together as you did with the lightweight wadding, butting the ends so as not to create bulk. Pin or tack (baste) to the wrong side of the bumper front.

8 Back the bumper by cutting four pieces of backing fabric 9½in (24.1cm) wide x width of fabric. Sew together along the short width and then cut to 165in (420cm) long (a little longer than front). With right sides together, pin to the front. Sew along all sides through all layers leaving a large opening in the middle, about 15in (38cm), for turning through. When sewing make sure your tie ends are not in your seams. Trim all wadding about ⅜in (1cm) from the raw edge and clip the corners. Reach into the opening and pull the entire bumper right side out. Press the bumper and turn the raw edges of the opening to the inside. With sewing thread, whipstitch the opening closed.

9 Use your sewing machine to stitch in the ditch through all layers on seams between the blue and off-white blocks. Place your finished bumper in position in the cot, using the ties to tie it to the cot slats.

>> Embroidery

- With three strands of blue stranded cotton, embroider a running stitch ¼in (6mm) away from every appliquéd star through all the layers (1).
- For the quilting, trace a large star and a circle on freezer paper. Iron the star to the centre of a blue square or rectangle. With your favourite marking tool, trace the star outline and then remove the freezer paper star. Iron the circle to the centre and trace around the circle. Remove the freezer paper circle. Repeat this for every blue square or rectangle. Embroider running stitch with three strands of blue stranded cotton on the stars and circles drawn. Remove marking lines when stitching is finished (2).

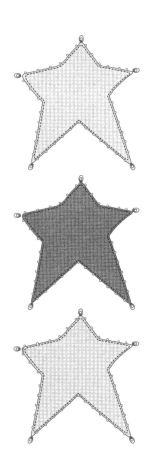

Rocking Horse Cot Quilt

An appliquéd rocking horse makes a wonderful centre panel for a cot quilt and the appliqué shapes are easy to apply. Alternating star and square-within-a-square blocks frame the centre beautifully. I used a soft minkee fabric for the backing.

You will need...

- Off-white fabric for quilt centre and block centres 1yd (1m)
- Four blue and four tan prints for blocks ¼yd (25cm) each
- Tan fabric for first border ⅓yd (30cm)
- Blue fabric for plaid appliqué ¼yd (25cm)
- Blue fabric for saddle and circle appliqués ¼yd (25cm)
- Two blue fabrics for circle appliqués and four yellow fabrics for stars ¼yd (25cm) each
- Three blue wool felts for star appliqués 18in x 18in (45.7cm x 45.7cm) each
- Tan and oatmeal wool felt for rocking horse appliqué 18in x 18in (45.7cm x 45.7cm) each
- Scrap of black wool felt for eye appliqué
- Large ric-rac braid 1½in (3.8cm) wide x 4yd (3.75m)
- Blue fabric for binding ½yd (50cm)
- Fusible webbing and freezer paper
- Light wadding (batting) 45in x 54in (114cm x 137cm)
- Backing fabric 45in x 54in (114cm x 137cm)
- DMC stranded cotton (floss) 813 blue, 3752 light blue, plus colours to match fabrics and felts

Finished size:
41in x 49in (104cm x 124.5cm)

>> Directions

1 Cut an off-white centre piece 20½in x 28½in (52cm x 72.5cm). To create the blue plaid appliqué, back the blue fabric for the appliqué with fusible web. For the plaid, cut three strips ¾in x 28½in (2cm x 72.4cm) and five strips ¾in x 20½in (2cm x 52.1cm). Start by fusing the centre vertical strip in place. Place the other two lengths about 4½in (11.4cm) from the centre strip and from the side edges and press. For the horizontal, place the strip in the centre and press. Now place two strips on each side of the centre about 4¼in (10.8cm) apart from each other. Place the last two strips about 4¼in (10.8cm) away from last two and from the top and bottom. The ends of strips should be flush with the edge of the off-white piece.

2 Add the narrow tan border by cutting two strips 2½in x 28½in (6.3cm x 72.4cm) and sewing these to the sides of the off-white centre, catching the blue strips in the seam. Press open. Cut two strips 2½in x 24½in (6.3cm x 62.2cm) and sew to the top and bottom, catching the blue strips in the seam. Press open.

3 For the rocking horse appliqué, trace the horse on to the paper side of the freezer paper. (The dashed line indicates where the horse shape continues under the mane and rocker pieces.) Press on to tan wool felt and cut out. Trace the mane, tail and rocker. (The dashed line is where the tail goes under the horse.) Trace the bridle, saddle, little star and circles on to the paper side of the fusible web. Press the pieces for the star and bridle on to the wrong side of the yellow fabric and cut out. Press the saddle and circles on to the blue fabric and cut out. Centre all these pieces on the middle of the quilt centre over the blue plaid following the design and overlapping where necessary.

Glue or pin the wool felts in position and then press the fusible pieces. Whipstitch in place with one strand of matching stranded cotton. Set this piece aside for now.

4 For the star blocks you will need to make nine blocks in total. Cut nine off-white centres 5½in x 5½in (14cm x 14cm). Each block needs a blue print border as follows. Cut two strips 2in x 5½in (5cm x 14cm), sew to the sides of the off-white square and press open. Cut two strips 2in x 8½in (5cm x 21.6cm), sew to the top and bottom and press open. Repeat on all the star blocks.

7 Sew the blocks together in the order shown in Fig 1 below. Press seams open.

Fig 1

5 For the square-in-a-square blocks you will need to make nine blocks in total. Cut nine off-white centres each 2½in x 2½in (6.3cm x 6.3cm). For the first blue border, cut two strips 2in x 2½in (5cm x 6.3cm), sew to the sides of an off-white square and press open. Cut two strips 2in x 5½in (5cm x 14cm), sew to the top and bottom and press open. For the second tan border, cut two strips 2in x 5½in (5cm x 14cm), sew to the sides and press open. Cut two strips 2in x 8½in (5cm x 21.6cm), sew to the top and bottom and press open. Repeat on all the square-in-a-square blocks.

6 To create the star appliqués, trace nine large stars and nine circles on to fusible web. Iron the stars on to your yellow fabrics and iron the circles on to blue fabrics. Trace one or two medium stars on to freezer paper. Cut out nine wool felt stars from different blues. Cut out large yellow stars and blue circles. Layer on each star block in this order: fuse a large yellow star in place, glue or pin a medium blue wool felt star and then fuse a blue circle to the centre of this star. Whipstitch appliqué edges with one strand of matching stranded cotton.

8 Trace the circles for the centres of the square-in-a-square blocks on to freezer paper and cut out. Press the circle on to the centre off-white square and with your favourite marking pen, trace around the circle. Peel off the paper and repeat for the other blocks.

9 Back the quilt with lightweight wadding (batting) and tack (baste) to hold the layers together. Embroider the quilt as described in the panel overleaf.

> **» TIP**
> *Freezer paper can be reused at least six times before it loses its ability to stick. Peel it off and re-iron on a new appliqué piece each time.*

10 Add the ric-rac by pinning it in place on the narrow tan border, pivoting neatly at the corners. At the ends, sew a French seam by first sewing wrong sides together. Trim close to the seam and then sew right sides together to finish. Press the seam. With your sewing machine, sew the ric-rac in place following the curve on each side to secure the braid.

11 For the backing I used minkee, which is a knitted fabric. Before using this it is necessary to back it with medium-weight interfacing to stabilize the fabric and prevent stretch. Follow the manufacturer's instructions to apply the interfacing. Tack (baste) the backing to the wrong side of the quilt. Bind the quilt with binding cut to your favourite width following the instructions in Binding a Quilt. I used a 3in/7.6cm width.

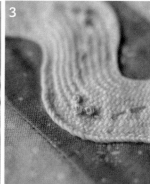

›› Embroidery

- With three strands of light blue stranded cotton, stitch a running stitch ¼in (6mm) away from the blue plaid strips (1).
- Use three strands of light blue and running stitch to outline the large stars and for the circles in the centre of the square-in-a-square blocks (2).
- Embroider on the ric-rac braid using three strands of light blue and running stitch. Stitch trios of French knots in blue (3).

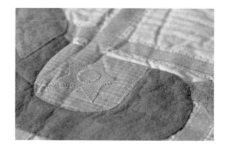

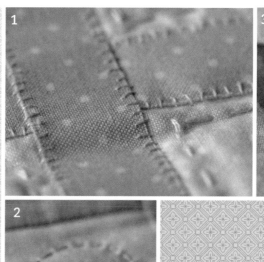

Sweet Memories

Collecting and displaying precious memories from childhood couldn't be easier with the projects in this chapter. Easy to make and very useful, they are made even more memorable with the cute little teddies used to decorate them. A wrap-around band adorned with little teddy faces is a really quick project, and versatile too – use it to secure a photograph album filled with memories or to wrap around a diary. Teddy bears are used as appliqués on a handy board, which is perfect for displaying favourite family snapshots. Doting parents and grand-parents are sure to appreciate a brag book to show off adorable photos of their little ones.

Pastel checked fabrics, lilac polka dot prints and lavender ric-rac braid bring a fresh colour scheme to all the projects in this chapter. The colourful appliqués are made easy with wool felt and fusible web.

Photo Album Band

This charming band with its fun teddies is perfect for wrapping around an album filled with precious photos. The idea could also be used for a cake band.

You will need...

- Lavender print fabric for centre ¼yd (25cm)
- Lavender ric-rac braid for border ⅝in (1.6cm) wide x 50in (127cm)
- Lavender wool felt for backing ¼yd (25cm)
- Scraps of wool felts for bear head appliqués (about 1½in/3.8cm square) in light pink, pink, light blue, blue, light yellow, yellow, cream and light green
- Lavender ribbon, two pieces each ⅝in (1.6cm) wide x 15in (38.1cm)
- Freezer paper
- DMC embroidery cotton in 310 black and 3863 brown, plus colours to match wool felt colours

Finished size:
4in x 21in (10.2cm x 53.3cm), excluding ties

>> Directions

1 See the Template section for the relevant templates. Cut two pieces from lavender print fabric each 3in x 20in (7.6cm x 50.8cm). Round the edges following the shape given on the template. With right sides together, sew all around leaving an opening for turning along the straight edge. Trim the seam, turn through and press. Hand stitch the opening closed.

2 Appliqué the bears by tracing one bear head and one muzzle on to the paper side of the freezer paper. Press the shiny side on to wool felt and cut out seven bear heads from pink, blue, green and yellow. Cut seven muzzles from the lighter of these fabrics, using cream on the green bear. Glue or pin the bear heads along the lavender print fabric about 1½in (3.8cm) apart. Whipstitch all appliqués in place using one strand of matching embroidery cotton.

3 Embroider the bears with two strands of brown embroidery cotton, satin stitching their noses and straight stitching a line for the muzzle. Work French knots for the eyes using two strands of black.

4 Tack (baste) ric-rac braid all around the fabric strip. At the ends, sew the seam right sides together and press the seam open to lay flat. Pin this fabric strip on to a lavender wool felt piece cut 5in x 22in (12.7cm x 55.9cm). Pin a length of ribbon between the fabric and the wool felt pieces at each end. Topstitch ⅛in (3mm) from the edge all around, catching the ribbon and the ric-rac in the seam. Finish by trimming the wool felt ¼in (6mm) from the ric-rac edge all round, echoing the shape.

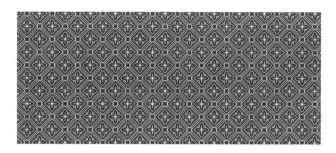

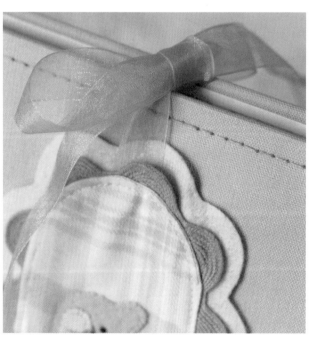

Memories Board

Sweet teddy bears decorate this easy-to-make board. It could be used to display favourite photographs in a child's room or for holding notes and reminders on everyday events.

You will need...

- Purple fabric for centre 19in x 19in (48.3cm x 48.3cm)
- Lavender print for border and criss-cross strips ¾yd (75cm)
- Light wadding (batting) 32in x 32in (81.3cm x 81.3cm) and 18in x 18in (45.7cm x 45.7cm)
- Wool felt for backing 24in x 24in (61cm x 61cm)
- Light green wool felt for bear appliqués 6in x 6in (15.2cm x 15.2cm)
- Wool felt for bear head appliqués in light pink, pink, light blue, blue, light yellow, yellow and cream 4in x 4in (10.2cm x 10.2cm) each
- Ribbon 1in (2.5cm) wide x 2yd (2m)
- Fusible web and freezer paper
- Cardboard 24in x 24in (61cm x 61cm)
- Corkboard 24in x 24in (61cm x 61cm) or four 12in (30.5cm) squares
- Hot glue gun and glue
- DMC embroidery cotton in 310 black, 3863 brown, 155 periwinkle, 581 green, 3821 light yellow, 3348 light green, 152 pink and 598 blue, plus colours to match wool felts

Finished size:
24in x 24in (61cm x 61cm)

›› Directions

1 Cut the centre from purple fabric 18½in x 18½in (47cm x 47cm). Cut the criss-cross strips as follows: two strips 1¼in x 27in (3.2cm x 68.6cm); four strips 1¼in x 16in (3.2cm x 40.6cm) and four strips 1¼in x 6in (3.2cm x 15.2cm). Turn under ⅜in (1cm) along the lengths to the wrong side (one edge will overlap slightly). From fusible web cut thin strips ¼in (6mm) wide and press under the overlap to hold in place on the back, which means they will not lift when photos are tucked under them.

»› TIP

Tacking (basting) the strips down stops them from lifting and being in your way as you work the embroidery and appliqué. Remove this tacking when the project is finished.

2 Place the strips in a diagonal manner on the centre fabric, with the longest two from corner to corner. The 16in (40.6cm) lengths are about 5in (12.7cm) from the centre on all sides. The 6in (15.2cm) lengths are about 5in (12.7cm) from the last four near the corners. I glued my strips down where they crossed to hold them in place (pins cause too much lift). Don't use too much glue, just a smidge, because the bear heads will go over this and you still need to sew these down and embroider. Allow to dry before the next step.

3 Attach the borders by cutting side border pieces 6in x 18½in (15.2cm x 47cm). Sew these to the sides of the centre piece and press open. Cut top and bottom pieces 6in x 29½in (15.2cm x 75cm). Sew to the top and bottom and press open. The border is a little wider to allow fabric to be overlapped at the back later. Tack (baste) the strips down by hand to hold them temporarily – see Tip.

4 Trace the embroidery lines for the border – see the Template section at the back of the book for the relevant templates. Tack (baste) the larger piece of wadding (batting) to the back of the project.

5 Appliqué the bears by tracing one or two bear heads and one or two muzzles on to the paper side of the freezer paper. Press the shiny side to the wool felt and cut out twelve bear heads from pink, blue, green and yellow. Cut twelve muzzles from the lighter of these fabrics (use cream on the green bear). Glue or pin the bear heads at the criss-cross points. Cut one large bear from light green. Use cream for the muzzle and feet. Place the large bear at the lower left corner. Whipstitch all appliqués in place using one strand of matching embroidery cotton.

6 Work the embroidery on the project as described in the panel, right. Remove the temporary tacking after the embroidery is finished.

7 Back just the centre of the project with the other piece of wadding to add a padding to the board. Prepare the cardboard by covering it with the 24in (61cm) square of corkboard. I glued mine on with a hot glue gun.

8 Centre the design on the board – it helps to use an iron and crease where it overlaps the edge (3in/ 7.6cm on all sides). Starting at the corners and using a glue gun, pull the corners to the back and glue them in place. At every corner check the front to make sure your design is still centred. Glue the sides and then the top and bottom.

9 Cut the ribbon into two lengths for a hanger. Glue these to the back, allowing at least 5in (12.7cm) to be glued on to the back for strength. Place the ribbons 4in (10.2cm) in from the sides, at angles pointing slightly towards the centre. Cut lavender wool felt 23½in x 23½in (59.7cm x 59.7cm) for a backing. Glue this to the back ¼in (6mm) in from all sides. Allow to dry. Tie the bow to the desired length, hang and fill with memories.

›› Embroidery

- Embroider the bears using two strands of brown embroidery cotton, working satin stitch for the noses and a straight stitch line for the muzzle. Using two strands of black work French knots for the eyes (1).
- Work the embroidery on the border using three strands of periwinkle cotton and a running stitch in a scallop shape. Work French knot dots with three strands of pink, light green, blue and yellow (2).

Brag Book

This lovely book is perfect for bragging to everyone as you show them photos of the latest addition to the family. Its concertina design allows for permanent display too.

You will need...

- Light print fabric for book ¾yd (75cm)
- Purple fabric for borders and tabs ¼yd (25cm)
- Light green wool felt for teddy bear appliqués 12in x 12in (30.5cm x 30.5cm)
- Wool felt for bear head appliqués 6in x 6in (15.2cm x 15.2cm) each in light pink, pink, light blue, blue, light yellow, yellow and cream
- Lavender ribbon ¼in (6mm) wide x 3½yd (3¼m)
- Six pieces of thin cardboard or heavyweight craft interfacing
- Fusible fleece ½yd (50cm)
- Freezer paper
- Four buttons ¾in (2cm)
- DMC stranded cotton (floss) 155 periwinkle, 310 black, 3863 brown, 152 pink, 598 blue, 3821 yellow, 3348 light green and 581 green, plus colours to match wool felts

Finished size (closed):
6in x 8in (15.2cm x 20.3cm)

≫ Directions

1 Start by making ten blocks for frames. Cut the centre pieces 3½in x 5½in (8.9cm x 14cm). On each of these mark 1¼in (3.2cm) from each corner. Pin and tack (baste) a 3in (7.6cm) piece of ribbon across each corner from mark to mark.

> **≫ TIP**
>
> *You could make one of the blocks of the brag book as a single frame for a special photo. Back it with cardboard and wool felt and add a loop of ribbon to hang it, as for the Memory Board.*

2 Add a border to each frame in lavender print. Cut two strips 1in x 5½in (2.5cm x 14cm), sew to the sides and press open. Cut two strips 1in x 4½in, sew to the top and bottom and press open.

3 To make the inside of the book cut five linking strips 2½in x 6½in (6.3cm x 16.5cm) from light print. Use five of these to sew the six frame blocks together alternately, beginning and ending with a frame block. Cut two ends for either side 1½in x 6½in (3.8cm x 16.5cm) from light print. Sew to the right and the left side along the 6½in (16.5cm)

length. Cut two strips 1½in x 36½in (3.8cm x 92.7cm), sew to the top and bottom and press open. The book inside is now a strip 8½in x 36½in (21.6cm x 92.7cm).

4 See the Template section for the relevant templates. With your favourite marking pen, trace lines for the spine on the inside. To the left and right of every lavender border, trace ¾in (2cm) away leaving a ½in (1.3cm) spine down the middle, from top to bottom. Trace the embroidery lines on the inside piece, tracing all the outside scallop borders and dots.

5 Back each frame block with fusible fleece cut 5½in x 8in (14cm x 20.3cm). Centre on to the back of each frame block, leaving the ½in (1.3cm) spine area free and ¼in (6mm) from the top and bottom.

6 For the outside cut three linking strips 2½in x 6½in (6.3cm x 16.5cm). Sew the remaining four frame blocks together alternately, beginning and ending with a frame block. Cut two strips for the top and bottom 1½in x 22½in (3.8cm x 57.1cm), sew to the top and bottom and press open. Cut two front and back pieces 7½in x 8½in (19cm x 21.6cm), sew to the right and left side of the outside along the 8½in (21.6cm) length. The outside will now be 8½in x 36½in (21.6cm x 92.7cm).

7 Trace the lines for the spine on this outside piece, as before. In addition, trace ½in (1.3cm) away from the first and last spine lines to mark the front and back pieces. Trace all embroidery lines. Back the outside with fusible fleece cut 8in x 36in (20.3cm x 91.4cm). Centre this on the completed strip ¼in (6mm) away from all edges.

8 Work the embroidery as described in the panel opposite.

9 Appliqué the small bears' heads by first tracing two heads and two muzzles on to the paper side of the freezer paper. Press the shiny side to the wool felt and cut out ten heads from a mixture of pink, blue, green and yellow. Cut ten muzzles from the lighter of these fabrics, using cream on the green bear. Glue or pin the heads in different places on each frame block, making sure they do not overlap into the spine area. For the book covers, trace the big bear on to freezer paper and cut two from green wool felt. Appliqué in place on the front and back covers. Trace a heart on to freezer paper and cut eight from pink wool felt and glue or pin in place. Whipstitch the edges of all appliqués using one strand of matching cotton. Embroider the bears as described in the panel opposite.

10 Make up the book as follows. Hand sew on the buttons – two on the front and two to the back, where marked on the template. With right sides together, sew the outside to the inside, making sure the bear heads are the right way up, sewing the sides and top only, leaving the bottom free. Clip the corners, turn out and press. Turn under ¼ in (6mm) along the bottom, press and pin together to hold. Slipstitch between the spine area only along the bottom to close. Topstitch by machine through all layers along all spine lines. Remove marking lines. Slip thin cardboard pieces (or heavy interfacing) into the openings, cut about 7¾ in x 5¼ in (19.7cm x 13.3cm) or to fit. Slipstitch these openings closed.

11 For the button tabs cut four pieces of lavender fabric 4½ in x 1¾ in (36.8cm x 4.4cm). Place two pieces right sides together and trace the tab shape on to the back. Sew all around leaving a small opening along the straight edge for turning. Trim, turn through and press. Slipstitch the opening closed. Make buttonholes on both sides of the tab to fit your buttons. Make another tab in the same way. The tabs are used to keep the book closed.

>> Embroidery

- With two strands of embroidery cotton work the running stitch scallop in periwinkle. Work French knots with two strands of blue, green, yellow and pink for the dots inside the scallop **(1)**.
- With two strands of brown cotton, satin stitch the small bears' noses and a straight stitch line for the muzzles. With two strands of black, work French knots for the eyes **(1)**.
- On the large bears, use three strands of the darker green cotton to work straight stitch claws and the running stitch seam line down the tummies **(2)**.

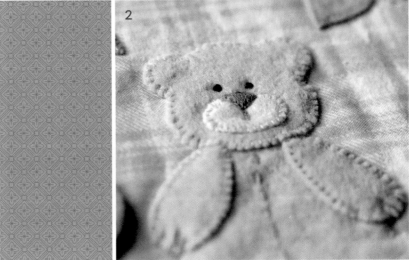

Going to Grandma's

When little ones are old enough to stay at Grandma's overnight it can be quite an event but the delightful projects in this chapter will make sure all goes smoothly. Bath-time at Grandma's will be great fun with a soft towel, its hood decorated with a cute rabbit in fluffy fleece. Just in case the little one misses Mummy, an ultra-soft blanket toy can be taken for comfort. It is made from fuzzy fleece complete with a sweet bunny toy. Everything needed for a stay at Grandma's can be packed into a roomy tote bag, and this one not only has eight useful pockets but is decorated with a charming little appliqué house and hopping bunnies.

Cream and pale green fabrics are the theme in this chapter, plus plenty of dear little bunnies and a sprinkling of hearts and flowers in easy wool felt appliqué. There are some opportunities for some lovely hand embroidery too.

Bunny Bath Towel

This towel looks simply adorable when finished, especially wrapped around a baby fresh from a warm bath. The rabbit template could be used for cot linen too.

You will need...

- Light green towelling fabric (terry cloth) 1¼yd (1.25m)
- Green print fabric for land piece 4in x 13in (10.2cm x 33cm)
- White fleece for bunny 6in x 9in (15.2cm x 22.9cm)
- Fusible interfacing 6in x 9in (15.2cm x 22.9cm)
- Green print for binding ⅓yd (30cm)
- DMC embroidery cotton (floss) in 310 black

Finished size:
30in x 30in (76.2cm x 76.2cm)

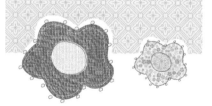

>> Directions

1 See the Template section for the relevant templates. Cut the towel from towelling fabric (terry cloth) 30in (76.2cm) square. Using the template, round all four corners. Cut an 11½in (29.2cm) square from towelling fabric and then cut on the diagonal for a triangle. You will only need one of these. This is the hood. Round this corner as well.

2 Cut a land piece from green fabric. Cut ¼in (6mm) larger across the top of the land piece if you plan to use a turned-under method for the appliqué. If using fusible web then cut to the size given. Appliqué the land piece to the towel hood, with the bottom edge of the land matching the long straight edge. I recommend using a zigzag stitch to hold if you are fusing, to strengthen this for washing.

3 Back the fleece with fusible interfacing to remove the stretch in the fabric before cutting out the bunny appliqué shape. Cut out the bunny shape, adding ¼in (6mm) if turning under, or to the size given if fusing. With three strands of black embroidery cotton, work a French knot eye where shown. Stitch the appliqué in place, using a zigzag stitch if fusing – see Tip below.

4 Bind the raw edge of the hood along the long straight edge. Cut the binding 2½in x 19in (6.3cm x 48.3cm). Fold in half with wrong sides together along the length. Match the raw edge of the binding to the raw edge of hood (the straight edge of the land). Sew ¼in (6mm) across. Turn the folded edge in place and blind hem stitch in position.

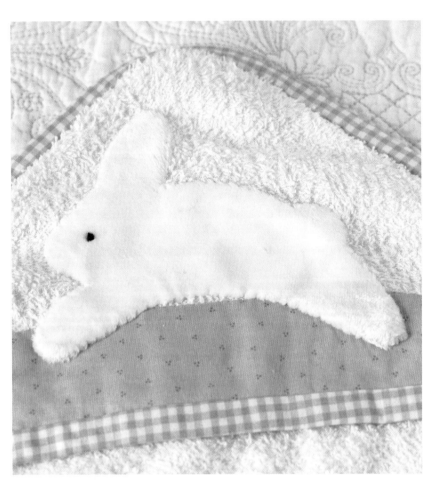

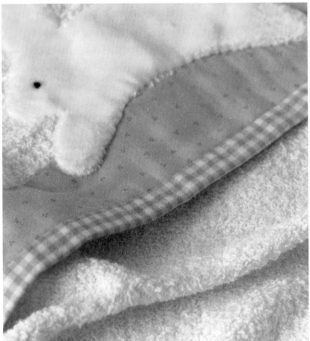

5 Pin the hood to a corner of the large towel piece, matching rounded corners and tack (baste) to hold. Cut three strips of binding 2½in (6.3cm) wide. Bind following the instructions in Binding a Quilt. Ease the binding around the corners with tiny tucks.

>> TIP

You could use fusible web for your appliqués. On a project that may need washing, anchor raw edges with a close zigzag stitch in a matching thread to create a finished edge. This will secure the appliqué and cause less fraying while washing.

Bunny Comforter

This comforter, made from fuzzy fleece complete with the cutest bunny toy, is wonderfully soft and is sure to become a treasured favourite for any little child.

You will need...

- White fuzzy fleece (minkee) ¾yd (75cm)
- Green fabric for backing ½yd (50cm)
- Off-white satin for binding ⅓yd (30cm)
- Off-white satin for bunny ears 6in x 6in (15.2cm x 15.2cm)
- Scrap of pink wool felt for nose
- Green fabric for heart appliqués 4in x 6in (10.2cm x 15.2cm)
- Fusible interfacing ½yd (50cm)
- Freezer paper
- Scrap fabric 5in x 5in (12.7cm x 12.7cm)
- Toy stuffing (fibrefill)
- Tweezers for turning and stuffing
- DMC embroidery cotton (floss) in 310 black, 224 pink, 581 green and blanc (white)

Finished size:
19in x 19in (48.3cm x 48.3cm)

›› Directions

1 See the Template section at the back of the book for the relevant templates. Start by cutting the blanket top from white fleece 18in x 18in (45.7cm x 45.7cm). Back this with interfacing the same size to eliminate the stretch in the fleece.

2 Cut eight hearts from green fabric. Cut the hearts ¼in (6mm) larger if you plan to use a turned-under method for the appliqué. If using fusible web then cut to the size given on the template. Appliqué a heart in each corner and centre of each side 1½in (3.8cm) from the edge. I recommend zigzag stitching the hearts down with matching thread if you are fusing. With two strands of green embroidery cotton, work a running stitch along the inside of the hearts.

3 Cut backing fabric 18½in x 18½in (47cm x 47cm). Find the middle of the top and back pieces and mark with a dot. Draw a 2in (5cm) diameter circle with your favourite marking tool. Tack (baste) these pieces together and with three strands of white embroidery cotton make a running stitch through both layers to quilt them together.

4 Bind the comforter with off-white satin cut 6in (15.2cm) wide. Mark ¾in (2cm) on the comforter on all sides. Line up the binding raw edge to this line and then sew in place. Trim the corners only. Turn the binding to the back and blind stitch in place.

5 Using the templates, trace the pieces for the head and arms on to freezer paper. Trace on the solid line, which is the cutting line. Cut these shapes from fleece by pressing the freezer paper on to the fleece and cutting out. Lay all your pieces on the fleece with arrows following the same direction (or nap) on the fabric. Turn the fabric over and lay these pieces on the other side to get mirror images if your fabric has a wrong side and a right side. Cut two face pieces, two back of head pieces, four arms and two ears. Cut two ears from off-white satin slightly larger than the size given. This helps because satin is slippery while being sewn down.

6 With right sides together, sew the face pieces from the top of the head to the neck as indicated on the template. Sew the back of the head pieces on the straight line as shown. Sew two arms together. Sew a fleece ear to a satin ear, placing them right sides together. Use ¼in (6mm) seams for all. I did not trim any seams. Turn ears and arms right sides out, using tweezers to help. Lightly stuff the arms by balling up a bit of stuffing and using the tweezers to stuff it in – not too much as we want the arms to be squeezable.

7 Pinch the ears in half with the satin in the pinch. With a threaded needle, anchor this pinch with a few stitches ¼in (6mm) from the bottom. Open the face piece and pin the ears in place on the face about ½in (1.3cm) from the middle seam with the satin side right side to face. Now open the back of the head piece. With right sides together, lay the back of head middle seam to the face middle seam and pin. Match neck edges and pin. Sew with a ¼in (6mm) seam from neck edge to neck edge. Turn right side out.

8 Trace the nose shape on to freezer paper and press on to a 1in (2.54cm) square of pink wool felt. Cut out on the solid line. Using a tiny bit of glue, stick the nose in place. Allow to dry and then closely whipstitch in place with one strand of pink embroidery cotton. With three strands of matching cotton, make a straight stitch from the bottom of the nose along the seam for ½in (1.3cm) and then work an open V shape at the end of this stitch. Using six strands of black embroidery cotton, work French knot eyes. I cut a tiny bit of scrap fabric and backed my fleece with it so the cotton had something stronger than the fleece to anchor to.

9 Stuff the head just enough to hold its shape. Using a 3in (7.6cm) square of scrap fabric, block the opening in the neck, pushing the fabric raw edges inside the head. Hand stitch in place to keep the stuffing inside. Hand stitch the arms in place, letting them extend under the neck edge a bit and pointing towards the face.

10 Pin the head in place on top of the quilted circle. With two long strands of embroidery cotton, hand stitch the bunny to the comforter top, just through the fleece. I went round and round for strength and through the arms too.

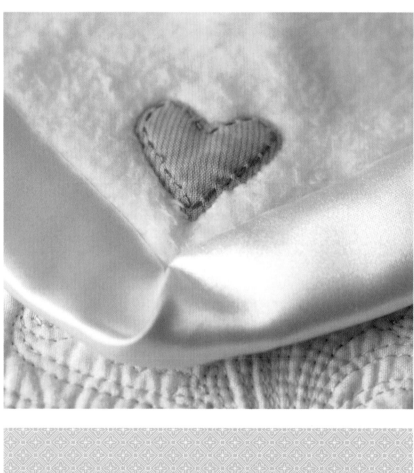

Little House Tote

Overnight stays at Grandma's will be great fun with this darling tote bag. The front and back are decorated with a delightful house scene, with large exterior and interior pockets, which make the bag very roomy. Smaller pockets are incorporated into each side of the bag too.

You will need...

- Two green print fabrics for bag outside and inside pockets ½yd (50cm) each
- Light green fabric for outside pockets ½yd (50cm)
- Green print fabric for bag bottom and land appliqué ¼yd (25cm)
- Contrast green fabric for lining ½yd (50cm)
- White, tan, light blue and yellow wool felt for appliqués 10in x 10in (25.4cm x 25.4cm) each
- Blue, pink, lavender, and off-white fabrics for appliqués 6in x 6in (15.2cm x 15.2cm) each
- Medium-weight fusible interfacing and fusible fleece ½yd (50cm) each
- Fusible web and freezer paper
- White ric-rac braid ⅝in (1.6cm) wide x 2½yd (2.3m)
- Cardboard and quilt wadding (batting) for bag bottom (optional) 5in x 14in (12.7cm x 35.6cm) each
- DMC embroidery cotton (floss) in 310 black, 167 tan, 224 pink, 581 green and 3821 yellow, plus colours to match appliqué fabrics and felts

Finished size:
13½in x 12in x 4½in deep (34.3cm x 30.5cm x 11.4cm) excluding handles

❯❯ Directions

1 See the Template section at the back of the book for the relevant templates. Start by cutting and preparing all of the outside pieces of the tote.

Cut two from outside green print each 14in x 12½in (35.6cm x 31.7cm) for the front and back.

Cut two from outside green print each 5in x 12½in (12.7cm x 31.7cm) for the sides.

Cut one from green print 5in x 14in (12.7cm x 35.6cm) for the base.

Back all of these pieces with fusible fleece cut ½in (1.3cm) smaller. Press the fleece on to the backs of the pieces with ¼in (6mm) space left all around for seams.

50.8cm). Fold in half wrong sides together at the 20in (50.8cm) length and press. The large pockets should be 14in x 10in (35.6cm x 25.4cm) and side pockets 5in x 10in (12.7cm x 25.4cm). Cut one piece for the bottom 5in x 14in (12.7cm x 35.6cm). Set lining pieces and inside pocket pieces aside for now.

5 Work the appliqué on the front pockets, using parts 1 and 2 of the template to trace the house, roof, cloud, flower centres and bunny on to the paper side of the freezer paper. Press the shiny side on to the corresponding wool felt colours. Cut two houses from tan, two roofs from blue, two clouds from white, nine bunnies from white and eight flower centres from yellow.

6 Trace two large land pieces, two small land pieces, eight flowers, four windows, two doors and two hearts on to fusible web. Press on to the back of the corresponding fabric colours. Press and cut two large green land pieces, two small green land pieces, two blue doors, four off-white windows, four lavender flowers, two pink flowers, two blue flowers and two pink hearts. Trace the embroidery lines on to your appliqué pieces and pockets.

7 Press the land pieces on to the pockets, with straight edges matching the raw edges of the pocket along the sides and bottom. This is so the edges get caught in the seams while sewing.

2 Prepare the pockets as follows. From light green fabric, cut four large pockets each 14in x 9¾in (35.6cm x 24.8cm). Cut two side pockets each 5in x 8½in (12.7cm x 21.6cm). Using the templates, cut curved edges along the top on these pieces. The solid line is the sewing line and the dashed line is the cutting line. Back these pieces with fusible interfacing cut ½in (1.3cm) smaller than the size given. Press the interfacing on the back with ¼in (6mm) space left all round for seams.

3 Prepare the bag lining by cutting two pieces from contrast green lining fabric each 14in x 12½in (35.6cm x 31.7cm). Cut two pieces for sides, each 5in x 12½in (12.7cm x 31.7cm).

4 Prepare the inside pockets by cutting two pieces from green fabric each 14in x 20in (35.6cm x 50.8cm). Cut two pieces for side pockets each 5in x 20in (12.7cm x

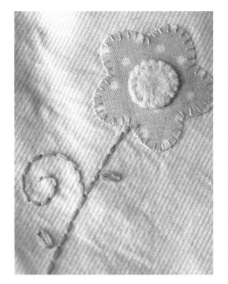

- Using three strands of embroidery cotton, work French knots in black for bunny eyes. With three strands of green, backstitch the stems and tendrils on the flowers and work lazy daisy stitches for leaves. With two strands of pink work French knots on all the dot flowers on the bunny collars (**1**).
- With three strands of tan cotton, backstitch the window panes and around the outside edges of the windows. Work French knots in tan for the doorknobs (**2**).
- With three strands of pink work lazy daisy petals on the flowers between the bunnies on the outside pieces and on the flowers on the doors. With three strands of yellow work French knot flower centres on the pink embroidered flowers (**3**).
- With two strands of green work backstitch stems on the flowers on the door and on bunny collars. Lazy daisy stitch all leaves (**3**).
- With three strands of pink work French knot dots around the hearts (**4**).

8 Glue or pin the wool felt houses and roofs in place. Glue or pin the clouds and bunnies in place on the pockets. Press all fabric appliqués in place and glue or pin yellow wool felt flower centres on top of the flowers.

9 Glue or pin bunnies to the outside prepared fronts and sides – three on each front and back, one on each side. Whipstitch all these pieces down with one strand of matching embroidery cotton. Work the embroidery on the project as described in the panel.

10 Make the pocket lining by placing the linings right sides together and sewing along the curved edge only. Trim and clip curves and then press the lining to the inside, matching raw edges at the bottom and sides. Trim if necessary.

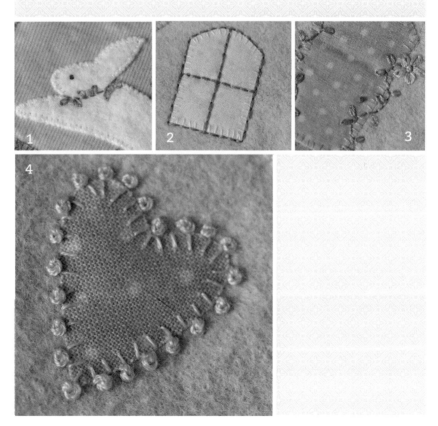

11 Cut two 16in (40.6cm) lengths of ric-rac for the pocket fronts and two 6in (15.2cm) lengths for the side pockets. Pin along the top curve. Tack (baste) through only the front piece to hold. Work embroidery through the front only, lifting the back lining out of the way while stitching. With two strands of pink embroidery cotton, work a French knot at every curve. With two strands of green, work lazy daisy stitch leaves.

12 Pin the finished corresponding pocket fronts to the outside front, back and sides, matching sides and bottom raw edges. Trim to make even if necessary.

13 With right sides together, sew the sides to the front starting at the top and stopping ¼ in (6mm) from the bottom (see Fig 1A). Sew the bottom to the front, starting and stopping ¼ in (6mm) from each side (Fig 1B). Press all seams open. Now sew the other front to the bottom, starting and stopping ¼ in (6mm) from the sides (Fig 1C). Sew the other front to the sides stopping ¼ in (6mm) from the bottom. Press all seams open. With right sides together, sew the gap in the bottom and sides (Fig 1D). Press on the outside.

14 To make the handles, cut two strips from green outside fabric each 3¼ in x 22in (8.3cm x 55.9cm). Press ¼ in (6mm) to the wrong side along the length. Press in half wrong sides together along the length. They should now be 1⅜in x 22in (3.5cm x 55.9cm). Cut two strips of fusible fleece each 1¼ in x 22in (3.2cm x 55.9cm). Open up the handles and stick fusible fleece inside under the ¼ in (6mm) hem and press in place. Pin the handles in place 2in (5cm) from each side seam on the bag front. Make sure the handles stick out at least ½in (1.3cm) from the top and that they are not twisted. Tack (baste) them in place.

15 Tack ric-rac to the bag top, matching raw edges. Overlap the ends and let them extend up and out, to be caught in the seam.

Fig 1A

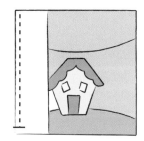

Fig 1B

Fig 1C

Fig 1D

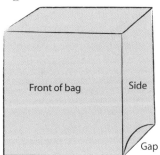

Front of bag Side

Gap

16 For the lining, lay the inside pockets on the corresponding lining pieces, matching sides and bottoms evenly. Trim if necessary and then pin or tack. Mark the large pocket division at 7in (17.8cm), to create two pockets on either side each 7in (17.8cm) wide. Sew through the pocket and lining piece from the top of the pocket to the bottom edge. Sew only one side to the lining leaving a 6in (15.2cm) gap between the pocket and the bottom when sewing – this will be a gap for turning right side out.

17 Sew the lining pieces with the pockets in the same way as step 13 (leaving the space in only one side). With the front of the bag right side out and the lining wrong side out, put the bag inside the lining. Match the top edges and pin. Sew all around, backstitching with your machine at the handles for strength. Trim, but not at the handles, leaving this extra length. Reach into the gap left in one side and pull the bag right side out. Press the top edges to the inside. Hand stitch the side opening closed. Topstitch ¼ in (6mm) from top on the outside to finish.

18 To make a firm bottom for the bag, cut cardboard 4¼ in x 13¼ in (10.8cm x 33.6cm). Glue a same size piece of wadding (batting) to this. Cut green fabric 4⅞in x 13⅞in (12.4cm x 35.2cm). With right sides together, sew the short side to the long side to the short side, leaving one long side open. Turn and press the long side seam to the inside. Insert the cardboard, hand stitch closed and place in the tote, padded side up.

Play Time

With young children in the house play time is all the time but fortunately the smallest of things can keep them happy and occupied for hours. The projects in this chapter do just that and make great gifts too. A set of soft blocks appliquéd with different geometric shapes are easy to make and ideal for young babies to play with. It's never too early to introduce children to the joys of reading and a fabric book with six charming farmyard scenes will be great fun for them to look at. A floor quilt made from fabrics with different textures, from smooth satin to fluffy chenille, will be a pleasure to play on.

The colours in this chapter are all pretty pastels, with fabrics that emphasize texture – perfect for little hands to grasp and explore. The use of simple geometric shapes makes the projects educational too, while the farmyard appliqué animals could be used on many other projects.

 **3-4 hour project**

Play Blocks

These blocks are perfect for a baby to play with and will help them learn their shapes. I used six different textures and seven different colours. Textures you might use include print cotton, chenille, fleece, satin and wool felt.

You will need...

For one block

- Six colours and textures for block 6in x 6in (15.2cm x 15.2cm) each
- Six colours for appliqué shapes 4in x 4in (10.2cm x 10.2cm) each
- Medium-weight fusible interfacing ¼yd (25cm)
- Freezer paper
- Heavyweight craft interfacing (Peltex) fusible on one side ¼yd (25cm) or ¼yd (25cm) of fusible web
- Craft glue
- Toy stuffing (fibrefill)
- Embroidery cotton (floss) to match wool felts

Finished size:
4in (10.2cm) cube

>> **TIP**
Wash all fabrics before using. Rinse wool felts in warm water to shrink and remove dyes and let them air dry before using. When the finished blocks need laundering, wash them by hand and allow them to air dry. A light cardboard could be used in place of the heavyweight interfacing but would not be washable.

>> Directions

1 Cut out six squares 4½in x 4½in (11.4cm x 11.4cm). Back the squares with interfacing (see Tip, right). With right sides together, sew squares 1, 2 and 3 together in a row with a ¼in (6mm) seam, pressing all seams open. With reference to Fig 1, sew square 4 to square 5, starting ¼in (6mm) from the top. Sew square 6 to the 4/5 set, starting ¼in (6mm) from the top. Sew square set 1/2/3 to set 4/5/6, sewing square 3 to square 5, starting and stopping ¼in (6mm) from the edges (Fig 2).

>> TIP

I backed all my blocks with medium-weight fusible interfacing before sewing. This served as a stabilizer for the light fabrics and took the stretch out of the stretch fabrics (fleeces) for ease of sewing. I also used it as a stabilizer for the stretch fabrics on the appliqués.

Fig 1

Sew square 4 to square 5, beginning ¼in (6mm) from the top

Square 4 | 5

Square 4 | Square 5 | 6

Sew square 6 to squares 4/5, beginning ¼in (6mm) from the top

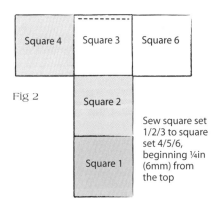

Fig 2

| Square 4 | Square 3 | Square 6 |

Square 2

Square 1

Sew square set 1/2/3 to square set 4/5/6, beginning ¼in (6mm) from the top

2 See the Template section at the back of the book for the relevant templates. To create the fabric appliqués, cut out the shapes ¼in (6mm) larger than given on the template, to allow for seams to be turned under. If using wool felt, cut out at the size given. Cut out these shapes using freezer paper and tracing the solid line. Glue or pin the appliqués in place and then hand stitch, using strong knots and close stitches for strength. I used the small circles, triangles, squares and heart shapes from the Fluffy Floor Quilt templates. Press all selvedges ¼in (6mm) to the wrong side. The finished layout will look similar to Fig 3.

3 Cut six squares 3⅝in x 3⅝in (9.2cm x 9.2cm) from heavy craft interfacing or Peltex. Back with fusible web if needed. These are cut slightly smaller to leave edges free for stitching. I added a little glue on the back of the appliqué for extra strength. Fuse to the wrong side of each square, over the turned-under edges and leaving a scant free edge all around each square.

4 Fold the block into shape. With a needle and long length of thread, anchor at the corners to hold in place while stitching. Leave one square free, like a jack-in-the-box top, for stuffing. Hand sew the edges together. Stuff the block with just enough stuffing to hold its shape. Hand sew the remaining square in place to finish.

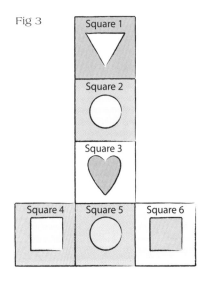

Fig 3

Square 1

Square 2

Square 3

Square 4 | Square 5 | Square 6

2 day project

Story Time Book

This soft book is a lovely way to introduce children to the joys of story-telling and reading. Simply make up your own stories around the six delightful farmyard scenes.

You will need...

- Blue fabric for book 'pages' ½yd (50cm)
- Green fabric for land appliqué ¼yd (25cm)
- Yellow print fabric for book spine 4in x 7in (10.2cm x 17.8cm)
- Medium-weight fusible interfacing ½yd (50cm)
- Wool felt for appliqué in light tan and white 10in x 10in (25.4cm x 25.4cm) each
- Wool felts for appliqué in ecru, light yellow, yellow, gold, oatmeal and black 6in x 6in (15.2cm x 15.2cm) each
- Wool felt for appliqué in red 2in x 2in (5cm x 5cm)
- Freezer paper
- Fusible fleece 6in x 18in (15.2cm x 45.7cm)
- DMC embroidery cotton in 167 tan, 310 black, 581 green, 739 light tan, 3042 lavender, 3761 blue, 3821 light yellow, 3830 red, 3852 yellow and blanc (white), plus colours to match felts

Finished size:
5½in x 6½in (14cm x 16.5cm)

›› Directions

1 See the Template section at the back of the book for the relevant templates. Mark six book pages on to blue print fabric with a fabric pen or pencil on the solid outer line given on the template. Back this with fusible interfacing for stability. Cut the pages if desired to work page by page or leave in one piece. If working page by page cut the pages on the solid line (a ¼in/6mm seam allowance is included).

2 Trace six land pieces on to fusible web and then fuse the web on to green fabric. Cut out the land pieces on the solid line. Press the land piece on to each page lining up the bottom and the page edge and ¼in (6mm) into the spine. Trace the embroidery stitches from the template on to your pages.

›› Embroidery

- Most of the embroidery is done with two strands of embroidery cotton except for the adult hen and rooster legs, which use three. All animal eyes are black French knots. All stems are green backstitch and all leaves are green lazy daisy stitches.

- Page 1 front cover: outline the window and door in tan backstitch, the big cross on the door in tan backstitch; alternate hay stitches in the window in light yellow and yellow straight stitches; hen wings in yellow lazy daisy stitch, tail and beak straight stitches in yellow; wheat seeds in alternate light yellow and yellow French knots; wheat stalks and leaves in green backstitch (1).

- Page 2: light tan French knot dots on sheep; lavender French knot dots on flowers; leaves in green lazy daisy stitch (2).

- Page 3: all chick fluff in light yellow straight stitches; chick wings in light yellow lazy daisy; chick and hen legs in yellow backstitch; chick and hen beaks in yellow satin stitch; hen spots in light yellow French knots; hen comb and wattle in red lazy daisy; daisy petals in white lazy daisy; daisy centres in yellow French knots; flowers stems in green backstitch (3).

- Page 4: cows' nostrils in tan French knots; tails in black backstitch; sunflower petals in light yellow lazy daisy; flower centres in tan French knots; flowers stems in green backstitch; leaves in green lazy daisy (4).

- Page 5: stems in green backstitch; leaves in green lazy daisy (5).

- Page 6 back cover: chick is the same as Page 3; dots on rooster in tan French knots, legs in yellow backstitch, beak in yellow satin stitch, tail feathers in tan fly stitch; daisy petals in white lazy daisy, flower centres in light yellow French knots (6).

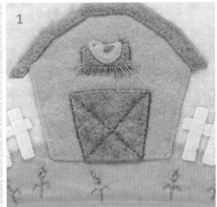

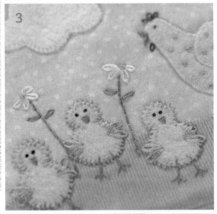

3 Cut out the appliqués by tracing the appliqué pieces on to the paper side of the freezer paper. Press the shiny side of the freezer paper on to the corresponding wool colours and cut out the shapes. Glue or pin the pieces into place and whipstitch the appliqués with one strand of embroidery cotton in colours to match the appliqués. The shapes and colours are as follows.

Page 1 front cover: barn in tan; door, window and roof in oatmeal; fence in white; hen in light yellow.

Page 2: sheep bodies and cloud in white; legs, heads and ears in black.

Page 3: cloud in white; chicks in light yellow; hen and wing in ecru.

Page 4: cloud and cow bodies in white; muzzles in ecru; spots in black.

Page 5: cloud in white; horse bodies in tan; manes and tails in oatmeal.

Page 6 back cover: fence in white; chick and sun centre in light yellow; sun outside in yellow; rooster body, wing and tail feathers in gold and comb in red.

4 Work the embroidery on the project as described in the panel on the previous page. See Working the Stitches in the Technique section for working all the stitches used here.

5 Cut three pieces of fusible fleece each 5½in x 5½in (14cm x 14cm). Back just three pages with this fleece – Page 1 front cover, Page 3 and Page 5, centring the fleece ¼in (6mm) from the page edge, top and bottom. Do not let this fleece go into the spine area.

6 With right sides together, pin the pages together as follows: Cover to Page 2; Page 3 to Page 4; Page 5 to Page 6. Make sure all spine sides are together and that pages are top to top and bottom to bottom. Sew on the dotted line around the top, the page edge and the bottom, leaving only the spine side free. Trim, turn right side out and press. Line up your pages, trimming at the spine if necessary. Tack (baste) with your sewing machine to hold the pages together through all layers.

7 For the spine cut yellow print fabric 3¼in x 6in (8.3cm x 15.2cm). Fold in half along the length, right sides together. Sew a ¼in (6mm) seam at the short ends. To create a hem edge fold back ½in (1.3cm) to the wrong side. Press and turn right side out. Check the fit on the spine; if it fits well, stick the spine of all the pages inside snuggly and tack (baste) in place. With three strands of blue embroidery cotton, make crosses through all layers to hold them together, making sure the back crosses are centred too. To finish, hand stitch the yellow fabric spine in place along the edge. All ready for story time.

>> **TIP**
Print fabrics could be used in place of wool felt. Back the fabrics with fusible web, trace the motifs and then cut out the shapes. Fuse the appliqués in place and then whipstitch the edges as you would for wool felt.

Fluffy Floor Quilt

Children will love this snuggly quilt with its different textures, from fluffy fleece and chenille to smooth cottons and silky satins.

You will need...

- Blue fabrics: print, chenille, fleece, satin ¼yd (25cm) each
- Pink fabrics: print, textured fleece, chenille, fleece, satin ¼yd (25cm) each
- White fabrics: textured fleece, print ¼yd (25cm) each
- Off-white fabrics: print, chenille ¼yd (25cm) each
- Green fabrics: two prints, fleece ¼yd (25cm) each
- Yellow fabrics: satin, fleece, print ¼yd (25cm) each
- Lavender print fabric ¼yd (25cm)
- Wool felt in pink, green and blue 12in x 12in (30.5cm x 30.5cm) each
- Medium fusible interfacing 4yd (3.75m)
- Freezer paper
- Backing fabric and low-loft wadding (batting) 1yd (1m) each
- Green fabric for binding ½yd (50cm)
- Off-white and green ric-rac braid ⅞in (2.2cm) wide x 1yd (1m) each
- DMC embroidery cotton (floss) in 3821 yellow, 152 pink, 813 blue, 3348 green and 3041 lavender, plus colours to match wool felts

Finished size:
33in x 33in (83.8cm x 83.8cm)

> **》 TIP**
> *All fabrics should be washed before use. Wool felts need to be rinsed in warm water to shrink and remove dyes. Let the felts air dry before using. The quilt should be washed on a gentle cycle when laundering is needed.*

>> Directions

1 See the Template section at the back of the book for the relevant templates. Refer to Fig 1 for the quilt layout, colours and fabric types to use. Start by cutting out sixteen squares each 8½in x 8½in (21.6cm x 21.6cm). Cut sixteen squares from interfacing the same size. Back the squares with the interfacing following the manufacturer's directions. Sew the squares together with ¼in (6mm) seams, four across and four down. Press all seams open.

>> **TIP**

The appliqué is worked using a turned-under method, so a seam allowance needs to be added to all shapes. This method is a more secure form of appliqué and will make the floor quilt more hardwearing.

Fig 1 Floor quilt layout

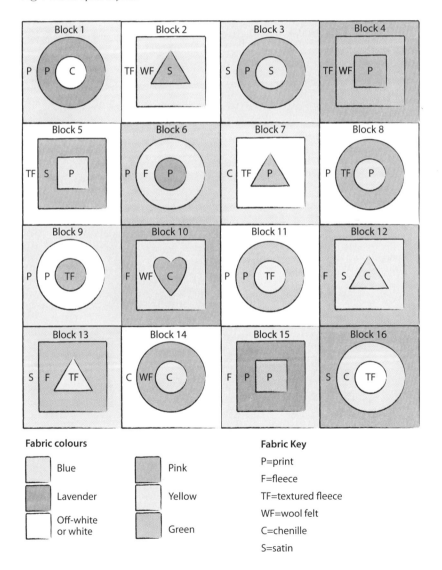

Fabric colours

Blue

Lavender

Off-white or white

Pink

Yellow

Green

Fabric Key

P=print
F=fleece
TF=textured fleece
WF=wool felt
C=chenille
S=satin

2 With reference to Fig 1, prepare the appliqués, cutting out eight large circles and eight large squares from your fabrics or wool felt. All appliqué is done by a turned-under method so cut out the shapes ¼ in (6mm) larger than given in the pattern. Wool felts are not turned under so cut out these shapes using freezer paper, tracing on the solid line given on the templates.

3 Appliqué a large circle or square to your blocks with matching sewing thread or one strand of embroidery cotton for wool felt appliqués. Make strong knots and close stitches to make the appliqués strong and secure.

4 Cut eight small circles for circle appliqués. I added ric-rac trim to five of the inside circle appliqués. Tack (baste) ric-rac to the circles after they are turned under but before the hand stitching is done, tucking the ends of the ric-rac under the circle.

5 Cut three small square appliqués, four small triangles and one heart. Hand sew in place where indicated in Fig 1.

6 Some of the blocks are quilted and decorated as follows. Use three strands of embroidery cotton for the running stitch. The ric-rac is anchored with French knot dots.
Block 1: green running stitches around large circle.
Block 3: off-white ric-rac around small circle and green French knots.
Block 4: yellow running stitches

inside small square.

Block 5: blue running stitches inside small square.

Block 6: off-white ric-rac around small circle with pink French knots. Yellow running stitches around large circle.

Block 8: green ric-rac around small circle, with yellow French knots. Lavender running stitches around large circle.

Block 9: green ric-rac around small circle and lavender French knots. Blue running stitch around large circle.

Block 11: pink running stitch around the large circle.

Block 14: off-white ric-rac around small circle and yellow French knots.

Block 15: pink running stitch inside small square.

Block 16: yellow running stitch around large circle.

7 Back the quilt with wadding and backing fabric. Use six strands of embroidery cotton in different colours to tie the layers together at the centre points – see Tying a Quilt in Techniques. Make a strong knot and trim the cotton to about 1¼ in (3.2cm) long.

8 For binding the quilt cut four lengths of fabric, each about 38in (96.5cm) long and 3½ in (8.9cm) wide. Bind the quilt following the instructions for Binding a Quilt or Cushion in the Technique section.

>> **TIP**

I backed my blocks with medium-weight fusible interfacing before sewing. This not only stabilizes the light fabrics but takes the stretch out of the stretch fabrics (fleeces) making them easier to sew. I also used it as a stabilizer for the stretch fabrics on the appliqués.

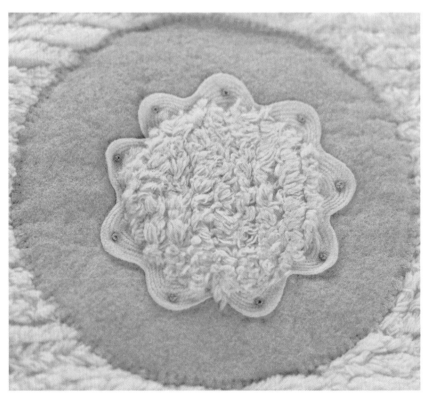

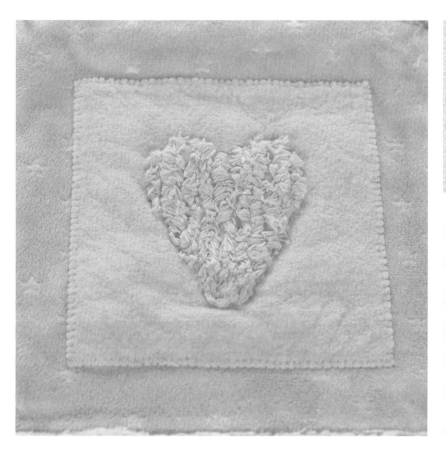

>> **TIP**

Use French seams on the ric-rac, as this will prevent edges fraying when the quilt is washed. Simply sew wrong sides together with a scant ⅛in (3mm) seam. Press the seam open, place right sides together and sew the seam again, catching the previous seam inside. The raw edges will then be inside and safe from fraying.

Basic Techniques

This section describes the basic techniques and stitches you will need to make the projects in the book.

Using this Book

- The projects in this book were made using imperial inches. Metric conversions are given in brackets but use *either* imperial *or* metric, as the systems are not interchangeable. The best results will be obtained using inches.
- All seams are sewn with a ¼ in (6mm) seam allowance, unless stated otherwise. Cutting instructions include a ¼ in (6mm) seam allowance.
- Appliqué design pieces are finished sizes. The appliqué templates do not include a ¼ in (6mm) allowance for turning under. If you choose to turn under your appliqué designs, add ¼ in (6mm) around the edges.
- The thicker lines in the templates are appliqué, while the thinner lines are embroidery.

Tracing Templates and Designs

Trace designs by centring them over a light source. This may be a light box or even a sunny window. Place your paper design to be traced first, then your fabric piece over this. It helps to tape your design in place so you can take a rest and come back to it if needed.

You can also trace the templates on to freezer paper and iron the paper on to fabric before cutting out – see Using Wool Felt, opposite. While it is more time consuming, it is precise. You can use the freezer paper many times. It is used on nearly all of the projects and is available in sheets or by the yard/metre.

Use your favourite tracing tool to trace designs on to fabric. Mine is a blue wash-away pen but you may prefer tailor's chalk, pencil or removeable pen.

Backing with Wadding (Batting)

I like to make my quilt tops and have them traced and ready for the embroidery work. Then I back my tops with a lightweight quilt wadding (batting) to create a 'quilted' effect while stitching. Cut the wadding larger than the quilt top, trimming it after all quilting is finished. You can hold the backing in place by pinning, tacking (basting) or with fabric spray adhesive, whichever you prefer. This method gives stability while stitching, allows the threads to carry over from point to point without the thread being seen from the front and, most importantly, plumps up the stitches so that they have body and are not flat.

Using Fusible Products

I have used various fusible products for the projects in this book, including fusible web, fusible interfacing and fusible fleece.

DOUBLE-SIDED FUSIBLE WEB

You will need fusible web for nearly all of the projects and it is available in sheets or by the yard/metre. It is often sold as Bondaweb or Wonderweb and can be used as a quick method of attaching an appliqué piece to a background fabric. One side looks like paper and you can trace the shape you want on to it (note that the shape will come out in reverse). Cut out roughly and iron it on to the back of the felt or fabric you want to appliqué. Cut carefully on the traced lines, peel off the paper backing and iron on to the background fabric to fuse, using a medium to hot iron. If you are using this method for wool felt appliqué, you can omit the whipstitch edging and move straight to the embroidery.

FUSIBLE INTERFACING

I have used single-sided interfacing on some fabrics, such as minkee and fleeces, to reduce the stretch and on flimsy fabrics to give them more body.

FUSIBLE FLEECE

Some fleece is available in a fusible form and I have used this for some projects, including the Brag Book and Little House Tote.

Using Wool Felt for Appliqué

Always pre-rinse your wool felts prior to use. Do this by running under warm water in the sink, rinsing until the water runs almost clear. Squeeze out excess water and allow to air dry before ironing. This will make sure all the dyes are out and that the wool is shrunk to size. It is good to get into the habit of rinsing felt as soon as you buy it. Store it by colour and it will be ready to use whenever you need it.

Use freezer paper to cut your wool felt design pieces. Trace the appliqué design on to the dull side of the freezer paper (there are no seams to turn under with wool-felt appliqué). With a dry iron, iron the shiny side of the freezer paper on to the wool felt and it will stick temporarily. Cut out on the traced lines and peel the paper from the wool felt. You can use the same freezer paper template many times.

Glue your wool felt appliqué pieces to your project – they only need tiny spots of fabric glue to hold them. This is a method I use with all appliqué. If you haven't done this before, you will love the fact that there are no pins to lose or threads to catch. After gluing, I press all pieces briefly with the iron. This anchors them and also makes the surface a little flatter and neater to whipstitch. Using one strand of embroidery thread matching the colour of the wool felt, I use a simple whipstitch (page 105) to sew to the background for a very neat look.

I use my favourite blue wash-away pen to mark embroidery lines on the wool felt. After stitching, I remove these lines with a very damp sponge, blotting the lines sparingly. Chalk also works well with wool felt and marks can simply be brushed away. Wool felt does not trace very well so I hope you become confident enough to apply the simple embroidery lines freehand. You will get very good at doing French knot dots and lazy daisy leaves on your own!

Binding a Quilt or Cushion

1 Cut lengths of binding fabric to a width of 2½ in (6.3cm). You may need to join strips together to make sure there is enough to go all round plus a few inches extra for the corners and ends. Fold the left-hand edge of the strip up to form a diagonal edge and press the binding strip in half, wrong sides together along the whole length (see Fig1A).

2 Pin the raw edge of the binding strip in place against the raw edge of the right side of the quilt, with the fold pointing inwards, 1in (2.5cm) or so away from the corner. Leaving the 1in (2.5cm) (the tail) free, sew a ¼ in (6mm) seam all the way along, stopping ¼ in (6mm) from the next corner (Fig 1B).

Fig 1A

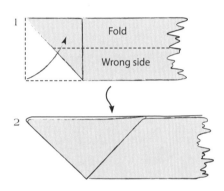

1

Fold

Wrong side

2

Fig 1D

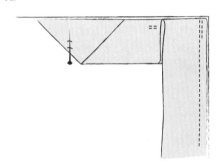

Fig 1B

'Tail'

¼in (6mm)

Raw edge

Fig 1E

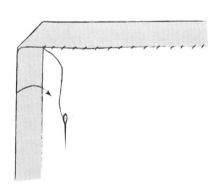

1

Fig 1C

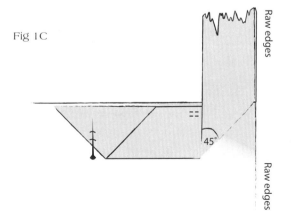

Raw edges

45°

Raw edges

2

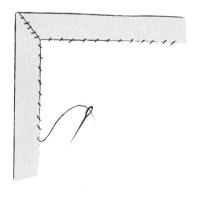

3   Fold the binding up from the corner to a 45-degree angle, keeping raw edges aligned, as shown (1C).

4   Fold the binding back down again to line up with the right-hand edge of the quilt (1D). Reverse stitch over the edge and continue sewing to within ¼in (6mm) of the next corner, then turn as before. When you reach the starting point, tuck the end into the folded tail and stitch over. Trim the wadding and backing even with the raw edge of the binding and quilt top. Trim corners on the diagonal to ease the fold of the mitred corner.

5   Fold the binding over to the back of the quilt and stitch in place, folding the binding at each corner to form a neat mitre as shown in the diagram (1E).

Tying a Quilt

The layers of a quilt can be tied with knots of thread at regular points instead of being quilted. Lay the quilt flat and smooth, right side up. Thread a needle with a long doubled length of embroidery thread. Put the needle in from the front of the quilt, through all layers to the back, leaving a 3in (7.6cm) tail of thread on the front. Make a small backstitch and come back through to the front. Tie off the thread securely with a square or reef knot and trim the thread ends to about ½in–1in (1.3cm–2.5cm) long. Make ties at regular intervals over the quilt, or according to the project instructions.

Using Embroidery Threads

For all the projects in this book I have used DMC stranded embroidery cotton (floss). These threads are widely available in a vast array of colours. In the embroidery sections of each project, I have indicated colours to use, but you can, of course, change these as you like or use a different make of thread.

Embroidery threads are usually formed from six strands and can be split into single strands. The number of strands to use for each piece of work (one, two or three) is indicated in the instructions for each project.

Working the Stitches

BACKSTITCH

Bring the needle up to the top of the fabric where you wish to start the backstitch line. Moving backwards, take the needle down ⅛in (3mm) away from the original hole. Bring the needle back up ⅛in (3mm) ahead of the original hole. Bring the needle back down into the original hole. Repeat this sequence, bringing the needle back up ahead of the last hole.

FLY STITCH

This stitch is essentially an open lazy daisy stitch pulled to a point. Bring the threaded needle up through the fabric. Take it back down ⅛in (3mm) horizontally from the beginning and back up again in the same motion ⅛in (3mm), centred and below, between the first two points. Catch the trail of thread loop while pulling to create a point. Bring the needle back down just over the cotton at the point to anchor.

FRENCH KNOT

Bring the needle up to the top of the fabric. Wrap the thread around the needle one, two or three times depending on the desired size of the knot. Put the needle back into the original hole, being careful not to let the loops unwrap. Pull the needle from the back, slowly drawing the thread through all the loops, creating a knot on the top.

LAZY DAISY STITCH

Bring the needle up to the top at the base of the stitch point (think of a teardrop – the base is the point, the round part is the loop). Bring the needle back down to the base in the same hole without pulling the thread all the way through. Let the thread make a loop and bring the needle back up to the top of the loop at the required distance from the base. Catch the loop with your needle and pull until the thread loop is the shape of a teardrop. Bridge the loop with a small stitch to anchor it in place.

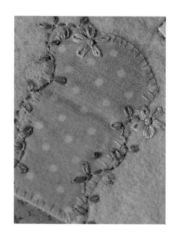

RUNNING STITCH

Bring the needle up to the top of the fabric. Make a stitch at the required distance (usually ⅛in/3mm) bringing the needle down. Bring the needle back up, again leaving a distance in between. Repeat until the line to be stitched is complete.

SATIN STITCH

Bring the needle up to the top of the shape you want to fill in. Bring the needle back down horizontally across the shape to the bottom. Bring the next stitch up right next to the first stitch, and then down, right next to the previous second stitch. Fill in with stitches snug against each other until the entire space is filled.

SLIPSTITCH

This stitch is used to close openings. Bring the needle to the front of one side a scant ¹⁄₁₆in (1.5mm) away from the edge. Catch the other side with a scant ¹⁄₁₆in (1.5mm) stitch. Draw up the thread bringing these two sides together. Bring the needle back to the original side and repeat, moving across the opening until it is closed.

TOPSTITCH

This is done with your sewing machine. Using a ⅛in–¼in (3mm–6mm) straight stitch, sew through all layers, anchoring your pieces to the backing fabric.

WHIPSTITCH

I used this stitch to anchor appliqué to the background fabric. Bring the needle up ⅛in (3mm) into the appliqué. Move the needle horizontally ⅛in (3mm) and down into the background fabric. On the wrong side, move the needle diagonally and forward ⅛in (3mm) up again into the appliqué piece and again ⅛in (3mm) down into the backing fabric. Repeat all around the appliqué shape.

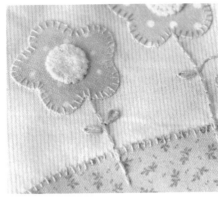

Templates

Important note: templates have been reduced by half so please enlarge templates by 200% on a photocopier before using.

Welcome Baby chapter
Large Bottle Wrap
Appliqué templates – *shown half size, so enlarge by 200%*

Small Bottle Wrap
Embroidery templates – *shown half size, so enlarge by 200%*

Welcome Baby chapter
Cutie Booties
Templates – *shown half size, so enlarge by 200%*
A seam allowance of ¼in (6mm) is included on all pieces

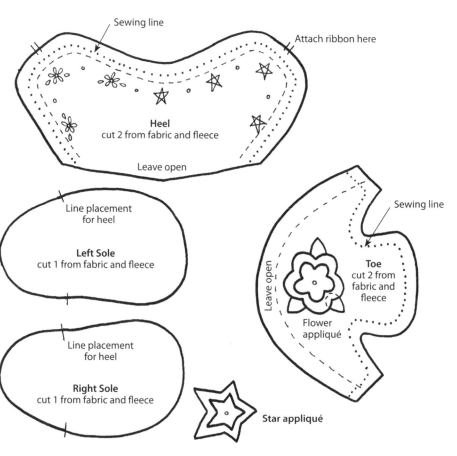

Sewing line

Attach ribbon here

Heel
cut 2 from fabric and fleece

Leave open

Line placement for heel

Left Sole
cut 1 from fabric and fleece

Line placement for heel

Right Sole
cut 1 from fabric and fleece

Sewing line

Leave open

Toe
cut 2 from fabric and fleece

Flower appliqué

Star appliqué

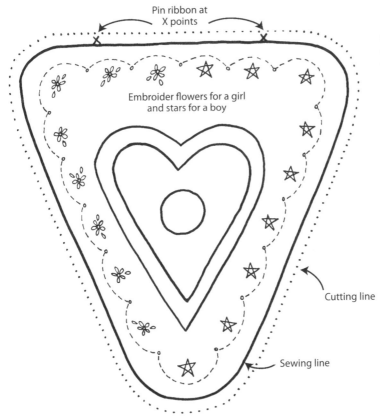

Pin ribbon at
X points

Embroider flowers for a girl
and stars for a boy

Cutting line

Sewing line

Welcome Baby chapter
Welcome Bunting
Templates – *shown half size, so enlarge by 200%*

Welcome Baby chapter
Welcome Bunting
Templates – *shown half size, so enlarge by 200%*
Dashed lines indicate where pieces overlap

Welcome Baby chapter
Sun and Moon Door Hanger
Templates – *shown half size, so enlarge by 200%*

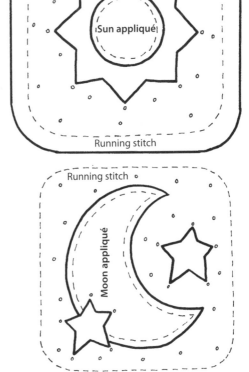

Place ribbon at Xs

Sun appliqué

Running stitch

Running stitch

Moon appliqué

Newborn Delights chapter
Armchair Caddy
Templates – *shown half size, so enlarge by 200%*

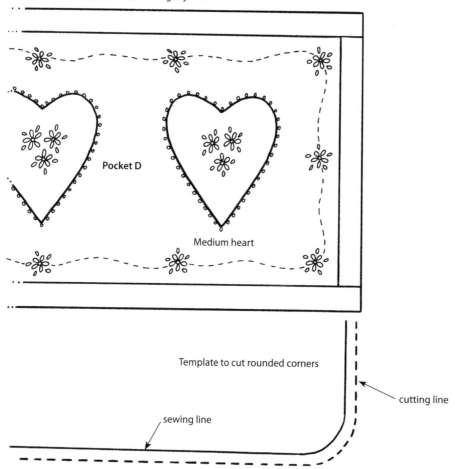

Pocket D

Medium heart

Template to cut rounded corners

cutting line

sewing line

Centre design of four hearts

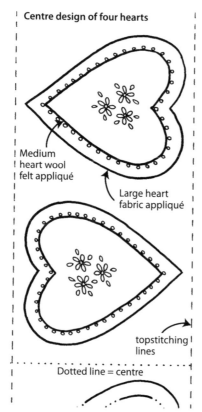

Medium heart wool felt appliqué

Large heart fabric appliqué

topstitching lines

Dotted line = centre

Newborn Delights chapter
Armchair Caddy
Templates – *shown half size, so enlarge by 200%*

Pocket B

Small heart wool felt appliqué

Newborn Delights chapter
Armchair Caddy
Templates – *shown half size, so enlarge by 200%*

Pocket A embroidery detail

Pocket C

Cut on solid
line – seam
allowance
included

Match at Xs

Match at Xs

Newborn chapter
Moses Basket
Liner templates (parts 1 and 2) –
shown half size, so enlarge by 200%

Match at Xs

Match at Xs

Total length =
27in (68.6cm) long x 10½in (26.7cm) wide

Beak

Newborn Delights chapter
Moses Basket
Appliqué Templates – *shown
half size, so enlarge by 200%*

Baby
head

Blanket

Stork body

Under wing

Top wing

Scallop trim –
cut two at 9½in (24.1cm) and
cut two at 30½in (77.5cm)

Clip

Clip

Clip

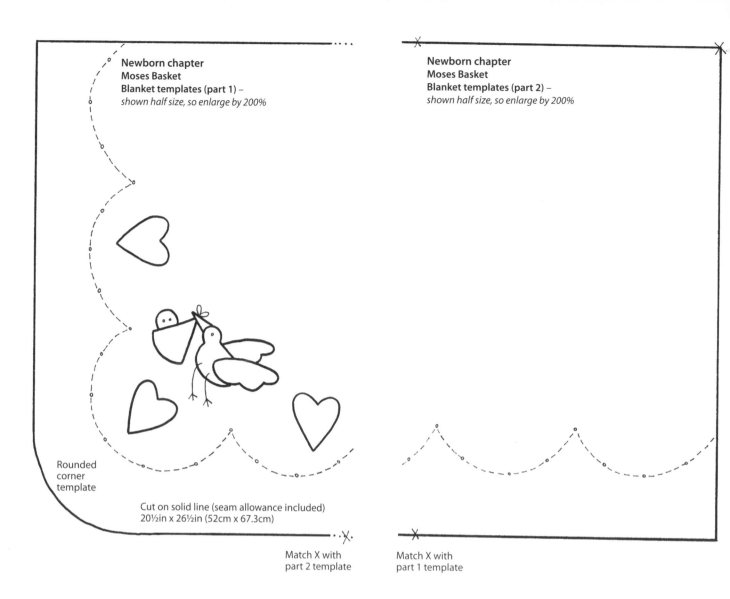

Newborn chapter
Moses Basket
Blanket templates (part 1) –
shown half size, so enlarge by 200%

Newborn chapter
Moses Basket
Blanket templates (part 2) –
shown half size, so enlarge by 200%

Rounded
corner
template

Cut on solid line (seam allowance included)
20½in x 26½in (52cm x 67.3cm)

Match X with
part 2 template

Match X with
part 1 template

Baby Girl chapter
Floral Wall Tidy
Flowers and Heart Pocket
Templates – *shown half size,*
so enlarge by 200%
Dashed lines indicate where
pieces overlap

Middle point – flip the template
to trace the other half

Baby Girl chapter
Floral Wall Tidy
Flower Scene Pocket
Templates (part 1) – *shown half size, so enlarge by 200%*

Baby Girl chapter
Floral Wall Tidy
Flower Scene Pocket
Templates (part 2) – *shown half size, so enlarge by 200%*

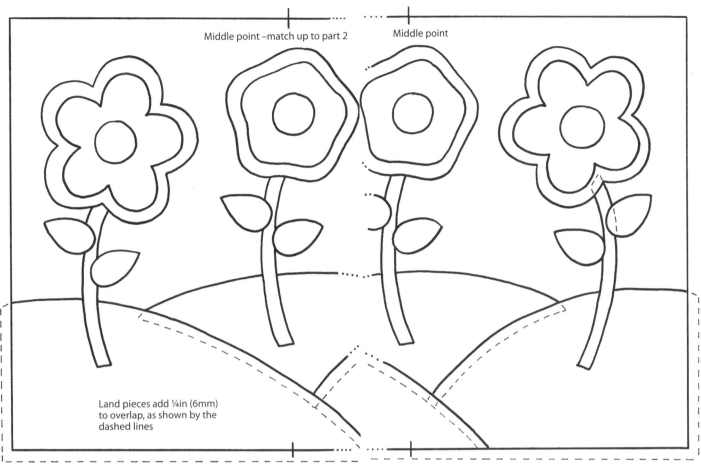

Middle point –match up to part 2

Middle point

Land pieces add ¼in (6mm)
to overlap, as shown by the
dashed lines

Add ¼in (6mm) to land pieces to catch in seam

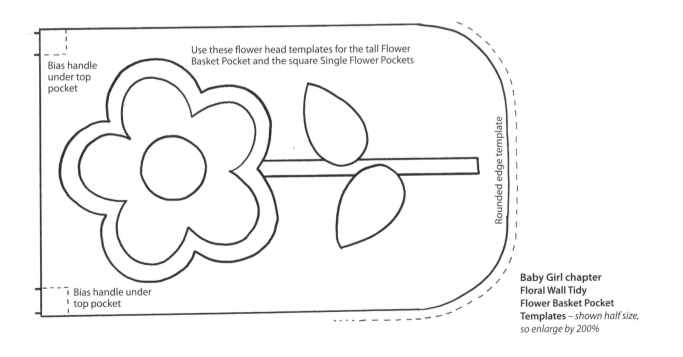

Use these flower head templates for the tall Flower
Basket Pocket and the square Single Flower Pockets

Bias handle
under top
pocket

Bias handle under
top pocket

Rounded edge template

Baby Girl chapter
Floral Wall Tidy
Flower Basket Pocket
Templates – *shown half size,
so enlarge by 200%*

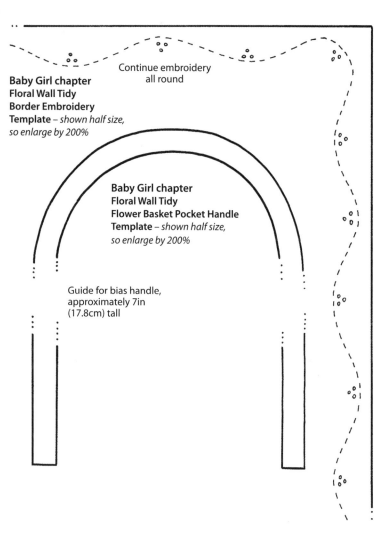

Continue embroidery
all round

Baby Girl chapter
Floral Wall Tidy
Border Embroidery
Template – *shown half size,*
so enlarge by 200%

Baby Girl chapter
Floral Wall Tidy
Flower Basket Pocket Handle
Template – *shown half size,*
so enlarge by 200%

Guide for bias handle,
approximately 7in
(17.8cm) tall

Baby Girl chapter
Flower Cot Quilt and Flower Decoration templates
– *shown half size, so enlarge by 200%*

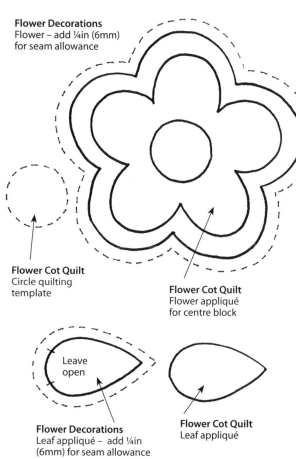

Flower Decorations
Flower – add ¼in (6mm)
for seam allowance

Flower Cot Quilt
Circle quilting
template

Flower Cot Quilt
Flower appliqué
for centre block

Leave
open

Flower Decorations
Leaf appliqué – add ¼in
(6mm) for seam allowance

Flower Cot Quilt
Leaf appliqué

Flower Cot Quilt – centre panel appliqué
The eight parts fit together as shown here.
Dashed lines indicate where appliqué pieces overlap.
Match the parts at the crosses.

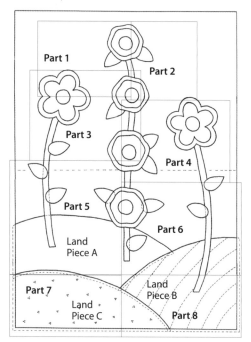

Part 1
Part 2
Part 3
Part 4
Part 5
Part 6
Part 7
Part 8
Land
Piece A
Land
Piece B
Land
Piece C

Flower Cot Quilt
Centre panel appliqué – Part 1

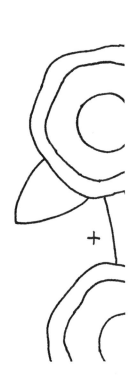

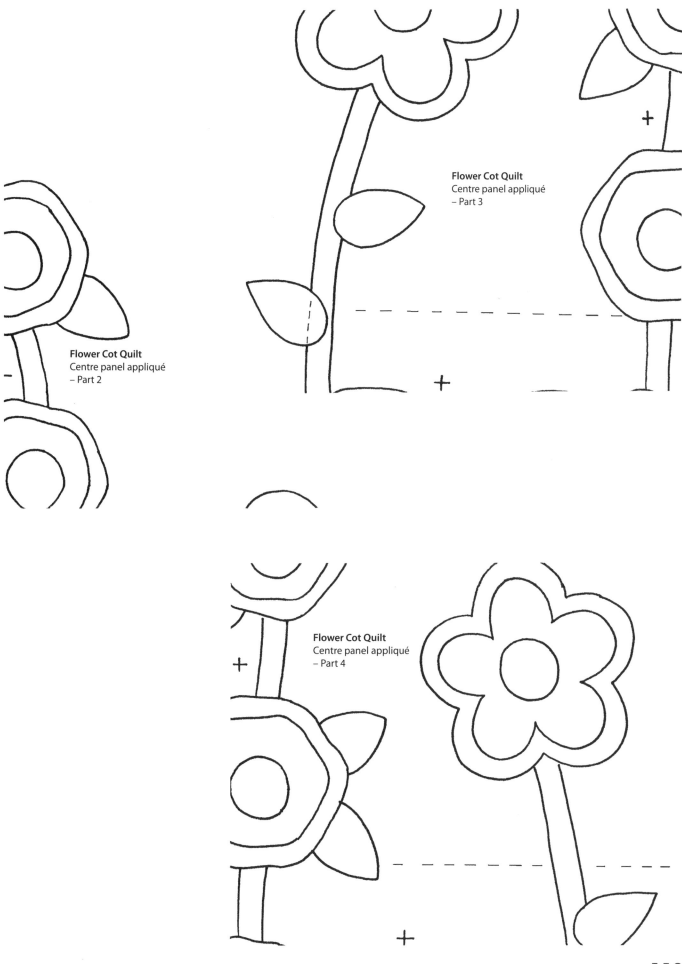

Flower Cot Quilt
Centre panel appliqué
– Part 2

Flower Cot Quilt
Centre panel appliqué
– Part 3

Flower Cot Quilt
Centre panel appliqué
– Part 4

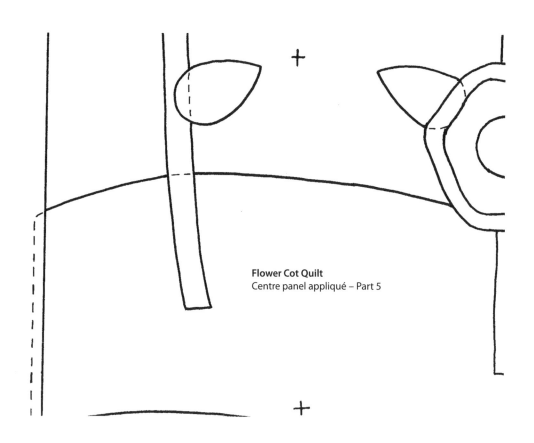

Flower Cot Quilt
Centre panel appliqué – Part 5

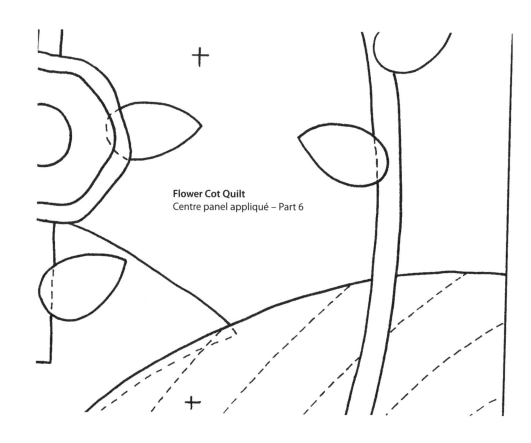

Flower Cot Quilt
Centre panel appliqué – Part 6

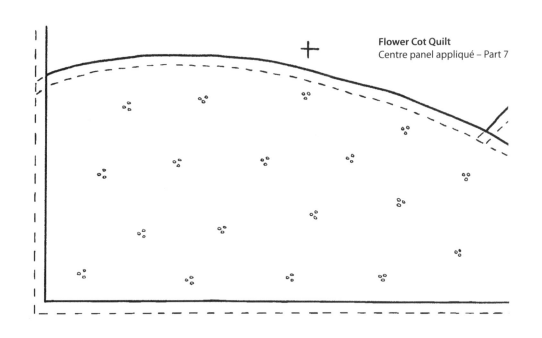

Flower Cot Quilt
Centre panel appliqué – Part 7

Flower Cot Quilt
Centre panel appliqué – Part 8

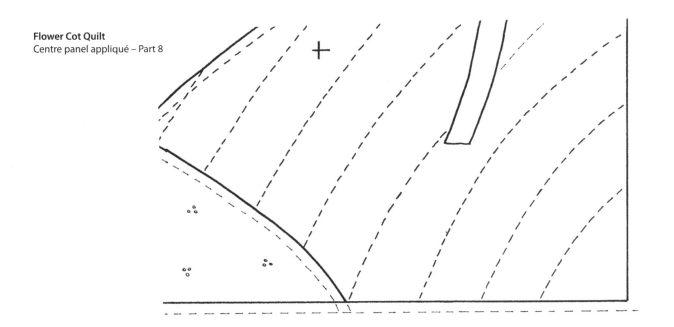

Leave open for hanger

**Baby Boy chapter
Nappy Stacker
Templates** – *shown half size, so enlarge by 200%*

Nappy Stacker top shape
cut 2 from off-white fabric placed on fold

cut on solid line and sew on dashed line with ¼in (6mm) seam

**Baby Boy chapter
Star and circle templates for Baby Boy Cot Quilt**
Cot Bumper and Pillow –
shown half size, so enlarge by 200%

quilting line

**Baby Boy chapter
Rocking Horse Cot Quilt
Appliqué templates** – *shown half size, so enlarge by 200%*

Match the pattern pieces at these dashed lines

Dashed lines indicate where design parts overlap

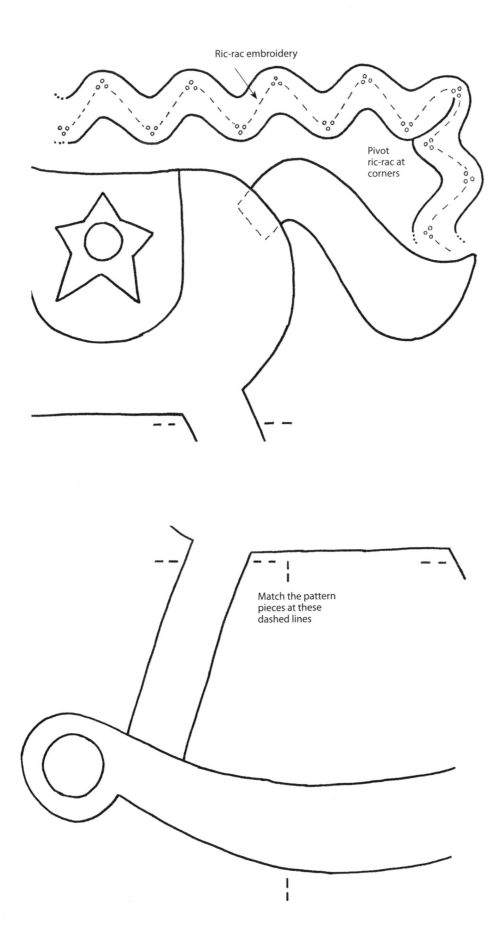

Ric-rac embroidery

Pivot ric-rac at corners

Match the pattern pieces at these dashed lines

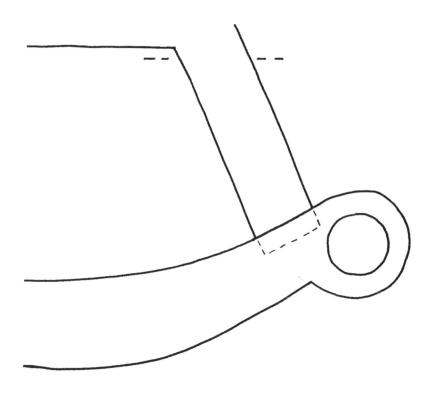

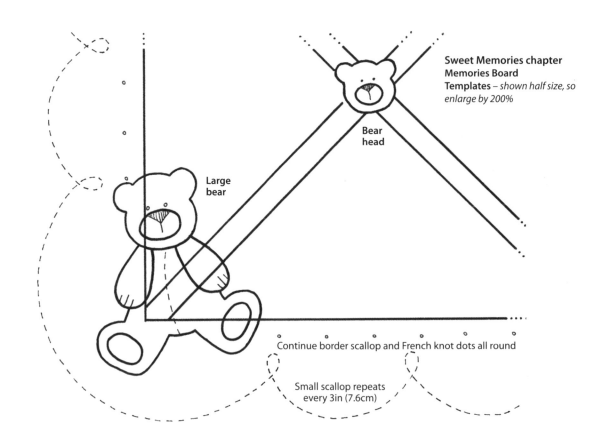

Sweet Memories chapter
Memories Board
Templates – *shown half size, so enlarge by 200%*

Bear
head

Large
bear

Continue border scallop and French knot dots all round

Small scallop repeats
every 3in (7.6cm)

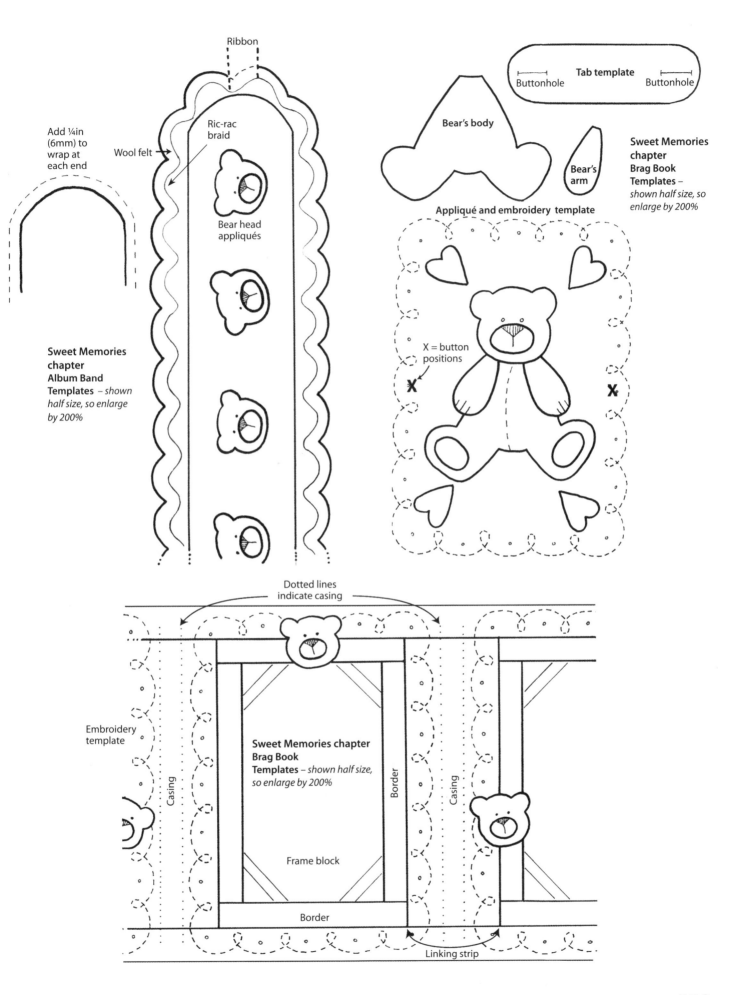

Ribbon

Add ¼in (6mm) to wrap at each end

Wool felt

Ric-rac braid

Bear head appliqués

Sweet Memories chapter Album Band Templates – *shown half size, so enlarge by 200%*

Tab template

Buttonhole   Buttonhole

Bear's body

Bear's arm

Sweet Memories chapter Brag Book Templates – *shown half size, so enlarge by 200%*

Appliqué and embroidery template

X = button positions

Dotted lines indicate casing

Embroidery template

Casing

Sweet Memories chapter Brag Book Templates – *shown half size, so enlarge by 200%*

Border

Casing

Frame block

Border

Linking strip

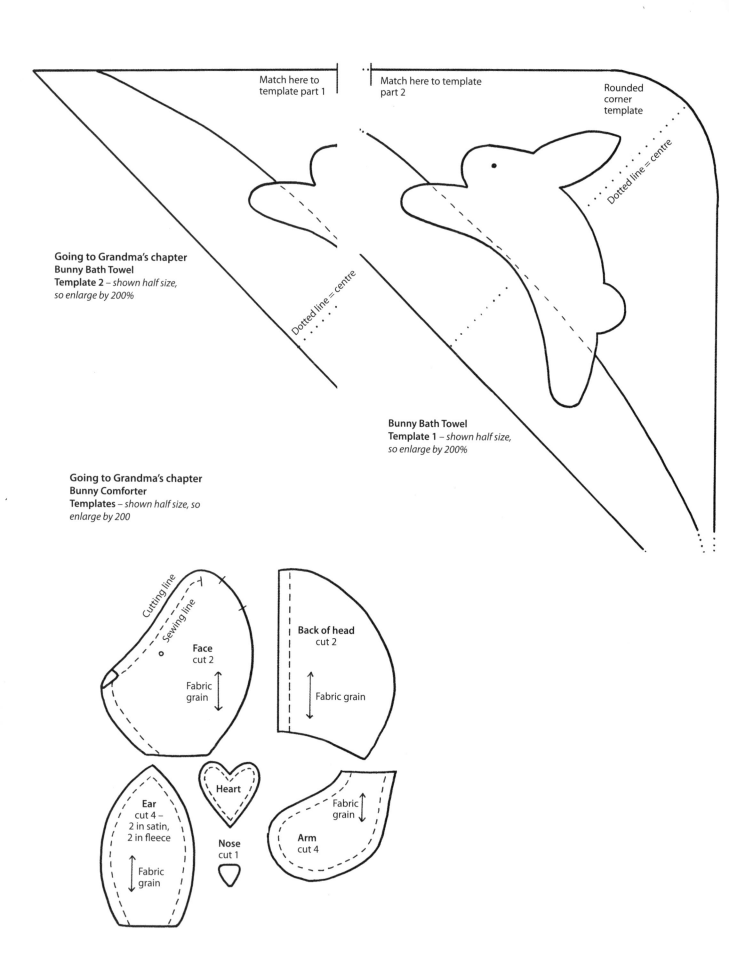

Match here to template part 1

Match here to template part 2

Rounded corner template

Dotted line = centre

Going to Grandma's chapter
Bunny Bath Towel
Template 2 – *shown half size, so enlarge by 200%*

Dotted line = centre

Bunny Bath Towel
Template 1 – *shown half size, so enlarge by 200%*

Going to Grandma's chapter
Bunny Comforter
Templates – *shown half size, so enlarge by 200*

Cutting line

Sewing line

Face
cut 2

Fabric grain

Back of head
cut 2

Fabric grain

Ear
cut 4 –
2 in satin,
2 in fleece

Fabric grain

Heart

Nose
cut 1

Arm
cut 4

Fabric grain

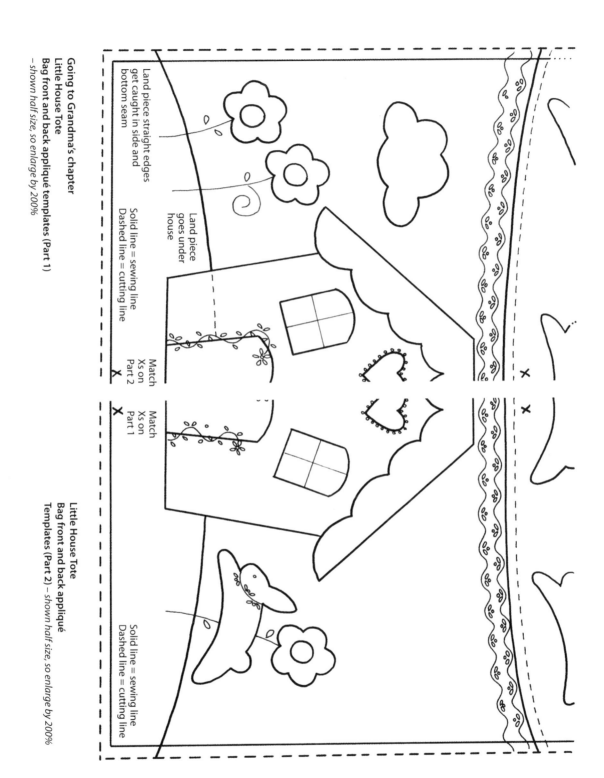

Going to Grandma's chapter
Little House Tote
Bag front and back appliqué templates (Part 1)
– *shown half size, so enlarge by 200%*

Land piece straight edges
get caught in side and
bottom seam

Land piece
goes under
house

Solid line = sewing line
Dashed line = cutting line

Match
Xs on
Part 2

Match
Xs on
Part 1

Little House Tote
Bag front and back appliqué
Templates (Part 2) – *shown half size, so enlarge by 200%*

Solid line = sewing line
Dashed line = cutting line

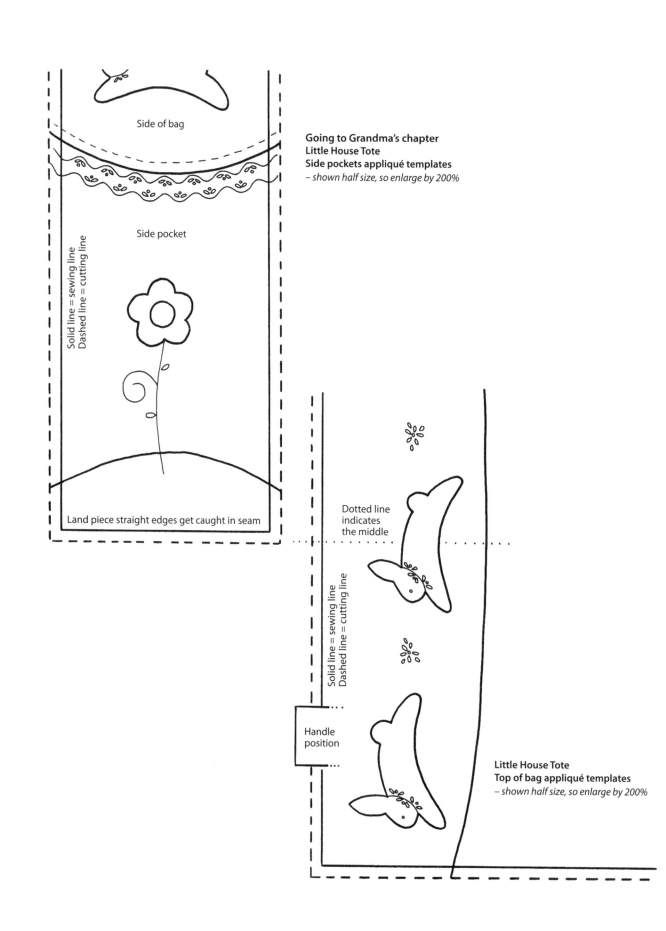

Side of bag

Going to Grandma's chapter
Little House Tote
Side pockets appliqué templates
– shown half size, so enlarge by 200%

Side pocket

Solid line = sewing line
Dashed line = cutting line

Land piece straight edges get caught in seam

Dotted line
indicates
the middle

Solid line = sewing line
Dashed line = cutting line

Handle
position

Little House Tote
Top of bag appliqué templates
– shown half size, so enlarge by 200%

Play Time chapter
Story Time Book
Page 1 front cover
templates – *shown half size, so enlarge by 200%*

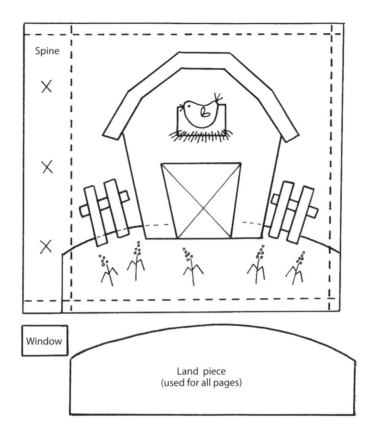

Spine

Window

Land piece
(used for all pages)

Story Time Book
Page 4 templates – *shown half size, so enlarge by 200%*

Spine

Cow head

Cow body

Calf head

Calf body

Play Time chapter
Story Time Book
Page 2 templates – *shown half size, so enlarge by 200%*

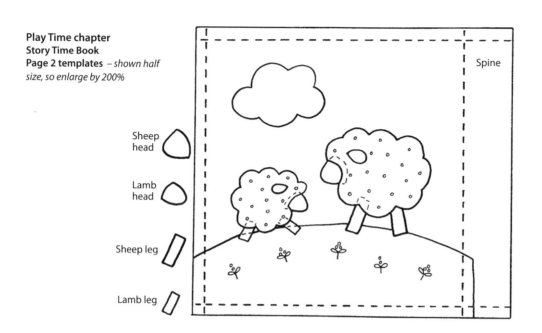

Sheep head

Lamb head

Sheep leg

Lamb leg

Spine

Story Time Book
Page 5 templates – *shown half size, so enlarge by 200%*

Spine

Story Time Book
Page 3 templates – *shown half size, so enlarge by 200%*

Chick body

Spine

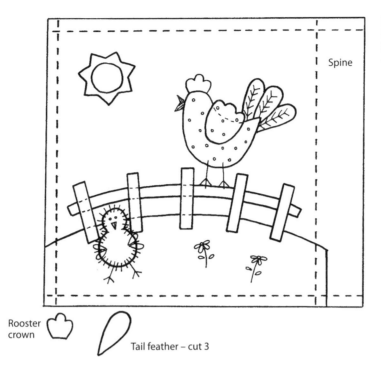

Play Time chapter
Story Time Book
Page 6 back cover templates
– shown half size, so enlarge by 200%

Spine

Rooster crown

Tail feather – cut 3

Play Time chapter
Floor Quilt and Play Blocks
Appliqué templates *– shown half size, so enlarge by 200%*
All appliqué shapes need to be cut out ¼in (6mm) larger to allow for a turned-under seam

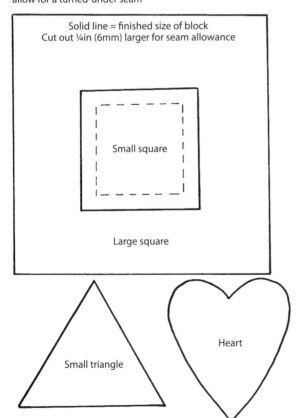

Solid line = finished size of block
Cut out ¼in (6mm) larger for seam allowance

Small square

Large square

Small triangle

Heart

Floor Quilt and Play Blocks
Appliqué templates *– shown half size, so enlarge by 200%*
All appliqué shapes need to be cut out ¼in (6mm) larger to allow for a turned-under seam

Running stitches around large circle

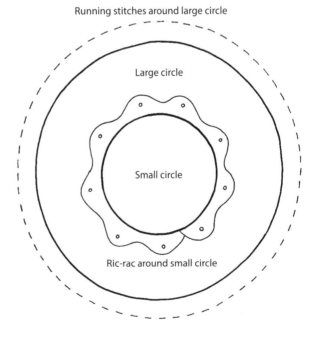

Large circle

Small circle

Ric-rac around small circle

SUPPLIERS

U.K. Suppliers

THE ETERNAL MAKER
89 Oving Road, Chichester,
West Sussex PO19 7EW
www.eternalmaker.com
For wool felt, haberdashery
and craft fabrics

- - - - - - - - - - - - - - -

WHALEYS
Harris Court, Great Horton,
Bradford, BD7 4EQ
www.whaleys-bradford.ltd.uk
For fabrics, and haberdashery.

- - - - - - - - - - - - - - -

JOHN LEWIS
Branches nationwide
www.johnlewis.com
For fabrics and haberdashery

U.S. Suppliers

BAREROOTS
www.bareroots.com
For a wide range of patterns by
Barri Sue Gaudet

- - - - - - - - - - - - - - -

HOMESPUN HEARTH
15954 Jackson Creek Pkwy, Suite B #546,
Monument, CO 80132
Tel: (866) 346 0414
www.homespunhearth.com
Online shop for fabrics, woven wools, wool
felt and needlecraft supplies

- - - - - - - - - - - - - - -

SIERRA COTTONS & WOOLS
2301 N. Sierra Highway, Bishop, CA 93514
Tel: (760) 872-9209
www.sierracottonsandwools.com
Email: sierracottonsandwools@yahoo.com
For wools, felts, fabrics, threads and kits

- - - - - - - - - - - - - - -

WOOL FELT CENTRAL
P.O. Box 184, Cozad, NE 69130
Tel: (308) 784-2010
www.woolfeltcentral.com
Email: prariepointjunction@yahoo.com
For fabrics, wool felts and kits (US only)

ABOUT THE AUTHOR

Barri Sue Gaudet has been around fabrics and crafts for most of her life. After many years of working in fabric and quilt shops, she began her own pattern company 'Bareroots' in 1999. She has enjoyed creating original designs of all kinds ever since. Barri Sue's designs include little quilts, cushions and stitcheries and are easily recognized by the delightful elements of nature and sweet little motifs contained in all. Along with the joy of her work involving what she loves, Barri Sue enjoys the opportunities to teach and meet others who love embroidery.

Barri Sue's other hobbies include knitting, painting, friends and being outdoors.

After raising two sons, Barri Sue moved to a tiny mountain town in the California Sierra Nevada Mountains named June Lake. She lives there with her husband Ron, a dog and two old cats. She has recently opened a stitchery and knitting shop in Bishop, California called Sierra Cottons & Wools.

Acknowledgments:

I would like to thank the David & Charles' team of Cheryl, Jeni, Lin and Jo. Cheryl for all her help with wonderful ideas, time management and support throughout creating this book. Thank you Jeni and Lin for your knowledge and thoroughness and to Jo for the lovely book design. You have all helped immensely and I appreciate it. I loved going back in time to remember having a little one in the house and would like to thank my babies Eric and Bryce for their inspiration.

INDEX